HEALING A PARENT'S
GRIEVING HEART

Also by Alan Wolfelt:

*Creating Meaningful Funeral Ceremonies:
A Guide for Families*

*Healing a Child's Grieving Heart:
100 Practical Ideas for Families, Friends
and Caregivers*

*Healing a Friend's Grieving Heart:
100 Practical Ideas for Helping Someone
You Love Through Loss*

*Healing a Teen's Grieving Heart:
100 Practical Ideas for Families, Friends
and Caregivers*

*Healing Your Grieving Heart for Kids:
100 Practical Ideas*

*The Journey Through Grief:
Reflections on Healing*

Understanding Grief: Helping Yourself Heal

Companion Press is dedicated to the education and
support of both the bereaved and bereavement caregivers.

We believe that those who companion the bereaved by
walking with them as they journey in grief have a
wondrous opportunity: to help others embrace and grow
through grief—and to lead fuller, more deeply-lived lives
themselves because of this important work.

Companion
P R E S S

For a complete catalog and
ordering information, write or call:

Companion Press
The Center for Loss and Life Transition
3735 Broken Bow Road
Fort Collins, CO 80526
(970) 226-6050
www.centerforloss.com

HEALING A PARENT'S GRIEVING HEART:

•

100 PRACTICAL IDEAS AFTER YOUR CHILD DIES

•

ALAN D. WOLFELT, PH.D.

Companion
PRESS

Fort Collins, Colorado
An imprint of the Center for Loss and Life Transition

Companion Press is an imprint of the
Center for Loss and Life Transition,
3735 Broken Bow Road, Fort Collins, Colorado 80526
970-226-6050
www.centerforloss.com

Companion Press books may be purchased in bulk for
sales promotions, premiums or fundraisers. Please
contact the publisher at the above address for more
information.

Printed in the United States of America

20 19 18 17 16   12 11 10 9

ISBN: 978-1-879651-30-2

And if I go, while you're still here...
know that I live on,
vibrating to a different measure
behind a thin veil you cannot see through.

You will not see me,
so you must have faith.

I wait for the time when
we can soar together again,
both aware of each other.

Until then, live your life to its fullest
and when you need me,
just whisper my name in your heart,
...I will be there.

Emily Dickinson

FOREWORD

Ever since the death of my beloved 17-year-old daughter, Judy, in 1976, my personal grief journey has brought me into close association with grieving people in every kind of circumstance. While every loss is important, bereaved parents universally report that the death of a child is the most challenging and difficult separation.

In 1977 I met Alan Wolfelt, and our friendship has deepened and matured over the years. He is one of the most respected grief educators and counselors in the world. As one of the rare individuals who can empathize with a situation outside his own personal experience, he offers practical wisdom and truly invaluable support as well.

In this conveniently small but powerful book, you will find common sense comfort and compassionate suggestions for virtually every experience the bereaved parent will face. Because the grieving mind is so dazed with shock, bewilderment and pain, each thought in this text is presented with brief clarity in everyday language.

Even after all these years, this book gave me fresh insights and renewed solace. Access to this kind of help in 1976 would have made a major difference in my grief. I would have draped this gem over a silken cord and work it around my neck 24 hours a day! So, whether you are recently bereaved or farther along in your journey, these 100 suggestions will shine new beams of sunshine and hope onto your path. I recommend one for your bedside table, one for your car, one for your desk and one for everyone who cares about you!

Andrea Gambill
Editor, *Bereavement* magazine

INTRODUCTION

I have learned that when your child dies, it's as if a deep hole implodes inside of you. It's as if the hole penetrates you and leaves you gasping for air. You bleed through the hole. As you mourn the death of your precious daughter or son, your agony slowly subsides, but never disappears. On the outside edges of that gaping hole, things begin to heal. Scars form. The hole is still present, but instead of only emptying out, it allows things to begin to enter in.

I hope the words I express from my heart throughout the following pages bring you some solace. I realize that no book can make your overwhelming loss go away. It rages in the recesses of your soul. Your profound loss will endure, and nothing I can say or do will alter that truth.

You have a broken heart. I truly believe that acknowledging your heart is broken is the beginning of your healing. As you experience the pain of your loss—gently opening, acknowledging and allowing—, the suffering it has wrought diminishes, but never completely vanishes. In fact, the resistance to the pain can potentially be more painful than the pain itself. Running from the pain of loss closes down our hearts and spirits. As difficult as it is, we must relinquish ourselves to the pain of grief. As Helen Keller said, "The only way to the other side is through."

Yet going through the pain of loss is not in and of itself the goal in our grief journeys. Instead, it is rediscovering life in ways that give us reason to get our feet out of bed and to make life matter. I'm certain you realize that the death of your child is not something you will ever "overcome" or "let go of." The death of your child doesn't call out to be "resolved" or "explained," but to be experienced. Experience relates to the "enforced learning of life." If anyone inappropriately tells you that "you will grow from this," remember the word ENFORCED. This is not growth you would choose. Actually, you would choose to have your child back in your loving arms!

So, who am I?

I am an author, educator and grief counselor who has been privileged "to bear witness" and learn from thousands of grieving parents, both at my Center for Loss and Life Transition and in my travels across North America. Over the past twenty-five years I have taught hundreds of workshops to groups of mourners and bereavement caregivers. I am also a husband to my wife, Susan, and a father to three beautiful children: Megan, who just turned a startling 13; Christopher, who is 11; and Jaimie, who is 6.

And, who am I not?

I am not a bereaved parent.

Members of The Compassionate Friends, an international organization for grieving parents, often say that their membership dues are the highest of any organization in the world. While I deeply admire and respect the work that The Compassionate Friends does in reaching out to "fellow strugglers," I hope never to join its ranks.

In this book, I speak to you not as someone who personally knows where you have been and where you might be going in your profoundly painful journey through grief. Rather, I speak to you as someone who has listened to the stories of thousands of grieving parents. Someone who has tried to "hold up" and "witness" these experiences to find nuggets of truth, hope, and healing. Someone who cares deeply about helping bereaved parents find meaning and purpose in their continued living.

I have been writing about grief and loss for more than two decades. For reasons I don't fully understand, a gap exists between having something to say and finally being able to pen something that even has a chance of being helpful to others. When I think of my efforts to learn from and support grieving parents, the time is now. I am ready to reach out and express what grieving parents have taught me in hopes of helping other parents who mourn the deaths of their precious children.

Please remember—the ideas in this book come from grieving parents. I have been their grateful student and they my patient teachers. I pass on to you their practical ideas for living after the death of a child in hopes that this book helps you survive what may seem unsurvivable and affirms that the many thoughts and feelings you are experiencing are normal. As Nicholas Wolterstorff wrote so honestly in *Lament for a Son*, "It's hard to keep one's footing." I hope that in a small way this book provides you some "footing."

Veteran grieving parents (an apt term, for surviving the death of a child is not unlike surviving the brutality and emotional and spiritual devastation of war) have taught me that they have survived and that they are once again glad to be alive. In many ways, this is perhaps the most important truth I have witnessed and want to pass on to you.

If you are a newly bereaved parent, I bring you the message that you will make it through this. Right now it may not seem so, but deep within us are emotional, physical, and spiritual layers that comprise our interior landscape. The death of your child has affected every layer within you. Over time and with the support of others, your grief will soften. No, it will never end, and it is likely that a day won't go by that you don't think about and miss your darling son or daughter. But, your grief will become less sharp and all-consuming. It will take on the blurred, bittersweet qualities of memory. On most days, it will murmur gently in the background while in the foreground, your life proceeds with purpose and happiness.

If your child died years ago, this book may affirm the journey that you have already taken. If you have felt "stuck" in some aspect of your grief, this resource may also provide you with new insights and ideas that will guide and support you. I have tried to bring you the experience and compassion of other longtime grieving parents in the hopes that your ongoing journey will be eased by their wisdom and their strength.

Whether your child was very young when he or she died or an independent adult, whether the death was the result of an illness, an accident, a homicide, or suicide, whether the death was sudden or lingering, the messages I am honored to bring you in this book are for you. There are 100 of them, and some will speak to your experience more precisely than others. If you come to an idea that doesn't seem to fit you, simply ignore it and turn to another page.

Some of the 100 ideas will teach you about the principles of grief and mourning. One of the most important ways to help yourself is to learn about the grief experience. The remainder of the 100 ideas offer practical here-and-now, action-oriented suggestions for embracing your grief and practicing self-compassion. Each idea is followed by a brief explanation of how and why the idea might help you.

You'll also notice that each of the 100 ideas offers a "carpe diem," which means "seize the day." My hope is that you not relegate this book to your shelves but instead keep it handy on your nightstand or desk. Pick it up often and turn to any page; the carpe diem suggestion might help you seize the day by giving you an exercise, action or thought to consider today, right now, right this minute.

While I do not believe in ranking losses in an attempt to define which kinds of losses are most painful and devastating to survivors, I have learned that grieving parents have a particularly difficult journey ahead of them. The death of a child may indeed create life's greatest upheaval.

But remember, you are not alone and your struggles are not forgotten. Millions of other grieving parents want you to know that you cannot only learn to survive but go on to discover renewal of meaning and purpose in your life. I am honored to pass along these resounding messages of hope and healing to you.

Finally, I have also discovered that no personal quality is more central to mourning the death of your child than courage. Courage is the ability to do what one believes is right, knowing that others may strongly disagree.

If people around you should try to persuade you to change the ways you are mourning the death of your child, stay steadfast. Trust your instincts.

I thank you from deep in my soul for having the courage to embrace the thoughts I've tried to express in this book. I hope we meet one day!

Alan D. Wolfelt

1.

KNOW THAT YOU WILL SURVIVE.

- All the veteran grieving parents I have ever had the privilege of meeting and learning from would want me to tell you this first: You will survive.

- If your loss was recent, you may think you cannot get through this. You can and you will. It will be excruciatingly difficult, yes, but over time and with the love and support of others, your grief will soften and you will find ways to be happy again. There will come a day when the death is not the first thing you think of when you wake up in the morning.

- Many newly bereaved parents also struggle with feeling they don't *want* to survive. Again, those who have gone before you want you to know that while this feeling is normal, it will pass. One day in the not-too-distant future you will feel that life is worth living again. For now, think of how important you are to your remaining children, your partner, your own parents and siblings, your friends.

- As time passes, you may also choose not simply to survive, but to truly live. The remainder of your life can be full and rich and satisfying if you choose life over mere existence.

CARPE DIEM:
If you're feeling you won't make it through the next few weeks or months, talk to someone about your feelings of panic and despair. The simple act of expressing these feelings may render them a little less powerful.

2.

KNOW THAT YOU ARE NOT ALONE.

- You are not alone. In the United States alone, more than 100,000 children die each year. (In other, less fortunate countries, of course, this number is staggeringly higher.) This number does not include miscarriages and stillbirths. Countless more adult children die; consider that most people who die in their fifties or younger leave behind a surviving parent. If you add up these numbers and consider all the children who have died in the last two decades, this means that literally millions of other parents are grieving the death of a child.

- I do not mean to diminish your unique pain. What matters to you, perhaps, is not that thousands of other children die every year but that your precious child has died. It is not the same. It is never the same.

- Still, even though your grief is indeed your grief and no one else was quite like your child, many other grieving parents have walked this lonely road. Reaching out to them, listening to them, and embracing their support and their messages of hope and healing will probably help make your grief journey more tolerable.

- The Compassionate Friends is the largest organization of grieving parents and its chapters hold support groups in hundreds of communities across the United States. Visit them on the web at www.compassionatefriends.org. Bereaved Parents of the U.S.A. (www.bereavedparentsusa.org) is another growing and reputable organization. For parents who have no surviving children, a group called Alive Alone (www.alivealone.org) may offer valuable assistance.

CARPE DIEM:
If you are ready and it feels right for you, look into support groups for grieving parents in your area.

3.

ALLOW FOR NUMBNESS.

- Feelings of shock, numbness and disbelief are nature's way of temporarily protecting us from the full reality of the death of someone loved. Like anesthesia, they help us survive the pain of our early grief. Be thankful for numbness.

- We often think, "I will wake up and this will not have happened." Early mourning can feel like being in a dream. Your emotions will need time to catch up with what your mind has been told.

- For grieving parents, feelings of passivity often go hand-in-hand with numbness. You may feel a child-like need to be fed, dressed, and led through the day. You may need others to make even simple decisions for you.

- Even after you have moved beyond these initial feelings, don't be surprised if they reemerge. Birthdays, holidays and anniversaries often trigger these normal and necessary feelings. Or sometimes feelings of shock and numbness will surface for no apparent reason.

CARPE DIEM:
If you're feeling numb, cancel any commitments that require concentration and decision-making. Allow yourself time to regroup. Find a "safe haven" that you might be able to retreat to for a few days.

4.

UNDERSTAND THE DIFFERENCE BETWEEN GRIEF AND MOURNING.

- Grief is the constellation of internal thoughts and feelings we have when someone loved dies. Grief is the weight in the chest, the churning in the gut, the unspeakable thoughts and feelings.

- Mourning is the outward expression of grief. Mourning is crying, journaling, creating artwork, talking to others about the death, telling the story, speaking the unspeakable.

- Everyone grieves when someone loved dies, but if we are to heal, we must also mourn.

- Many of the ideas in this book are intended to help you mourn the death of your child, to express your grief outside of yourself. Over time, and with the support of others, to mourn is to heal.

CARPE DIEM:
Ask yourself this: Have I truly been mourning the death of my child or have I restricted myself to grieving?

5.

BE COMPASSIONATE
WITH YOURSELF.

- The journey through grief is a long and difficult one, especially for parents whose child has died. This death is wrong—it is unnatural, it is out of order, it is unfair, it is unfathomable.

- Be compassionate with yourself as you encounter painful thoughts and feelings. Allow yourself to think and do whatever you need to think and do to survive.

- Don't judge yourself or try to set a particular course for healing. There is no single, right way to grieve and there is no timetable.

- Let your journey be what it is. And let yourself—your new, grieving self—be who you are.

- If others judge you or try to direct your grief in ways that seem hurtful or inappropriate, ignore them. You are the only expert of your grief. Usually such people are well-intentioned but they lack insight. See if you can muster some compassion for them, too.

CARPE DIEM:
What are you beating yourself up about these days? If you have the energy (and you won't always), address the problem head-on. If you can do something about it, do it. If you can't, try to be self-forgiving.

6.

BE COMPASSIONATE
WITH YOUR SPOUSE.

- Someone else is grieving this death as deeply as you are. Unless you are widowed or a single parent, the child's other parent is also mired in grief. Be as compassionate and nonjudgmental as you can be about your partner's reactions to the death. Give each other permission to mourn differently.

- Grieving parents are often not able to support one another well in the early weeks and months of their grief. They are simply too overcome with their own thoughts and feelings to be truly helpful to someone else. This is normal and not a marital failure.

- Mothers sometimes feel that they are more affected by the death of a child. In fact, some research has shown that a mother's grief is more disabling and longer-lasting. Yet the intensity of feeling often depends most on the parent's closeness to the child, not on gender. Fathers often feel the same depths of grief when a child dies, though these feelings are sometimes not expressed.

- Largely due to societal norms and expectations, fathers and mothers tend to mourn differently. Men often appear to be more stoic, and they may want to return to work faster. Women are typically more outwardly emotional and slower to return to daily routines. Yet in some marriages, these roles seem to be reversed. All these responses are normal and are not a gauge of the parent's love for the child who died.

CARPE DIEM:
Today, plan a time to talk to your partner about your
child and any unreconciled feelings you have toward him or her
regarding the death, even if the death was long ago. Your goal
is not to accuse or judge but rather to listen and to love.

7.

BE COMPASSIONATE WITH YOUR SURVIVING CHILDREN.

- Grieving siblings are often "forgotten mourners." This means that their parents and family as well as friends and society tend to overlook their ongoing grief or attempt to soothe it away.

- What grieving siblings really need is for adults to be open and honest with them about the death. And they need to know that their grief is important, too, and that their unique thoughts and feelings are acknowledged.

- Share your grief with your surviving children and make time to understand theirs. They must be your priority. If you just can't make yourself emotionally available right now, gently explain this to the child and appoint another adult as grief helper for the time-being.

- Don't put your surviving children in the position of having to parent you. Be honest with them about your grief but do not expect them to be your main source of comfort.

- On the other hand, try not to let your grief consume your household day in and day out. Your surviving children have many daily needs—school, activities, nutrition, hygiene, birthdays and other special occasions. Your home should still be a sanctuary for your surviving children. If you simply cannot attend to your children's needs right now, appoint other family members and friends to help.

CARPE DIEM:
Hold a family meeting and talk to your children about their feelings since the death. Even if the death wasn't recent, you may uncover lingering resentments, fears and regrets. Expressing these feelings may help bring your family closer together.

8.

UNDERSTAND THE SIX NEEDS OF MOURNING

Need #1: Acknowledge the reality of the death.

- Your child has died. This is probably the most difficult reality in the world to accept. Yet gently, slowly and patiently you must embrace this reality, bit by bit, day by day.

- Whether your child's death was sudden or anticipated, acknowledging the full reality of the loss may occur over weeks, months, even years.

- You will first acknowledge the reality of the loss with your head. Only over time will you come to acknowledge it with your heart.

- At times you may push away the reality of the death. This is normal and necessary for your survival. You will come to integrate the reality in doses as you are ready.

CARPE DIEM:
Tell someone about your child today. Talking about both the life and the death will help you work on this important need.

9.

UNDERSTAND THE SIX
NEEDS OF MOURNING

Need #2: Embrace the pain of the loss.

• This need requires mourners to embrace the pain of their loss—
something we naturally don't want to do. It is easier to avoid,
repress or push away the pain of grief than it is to confront it.

• It is in embracing your grief, however, that you will learn to
reconcile yourself to it.

• In the early days after the death of your child, your pain may seem
ever-present. Your every thought and feeling, every moment of
every day, may seem painful. During this time, you will probably
need to seek refuge from your pain. Go for a walk, read a book,
watch TV, talk to supportive friends and family about the normal
things of everyday life.

• While you do need to embrace the pain of your loss, you must do it
in doses, over time. You simply cannot take in the enormity of your
loss all at once. It's healthy to seek distractions and allow yourself
bits of pleasure each day.

CARPE DIEM:
If you feel up to it, allow yourself a time for embracing
pain today. Dedicate 15 minutes to thinking about and feeling
the loss. Reach out to someone who doesn't try to take your
pain away and spend some time with him.

10.

UNDERSTAND THE SIX NEEDS OF MOURNING

Need #3: Remember the person who died.

• When someone loved dies, they live on in us through memory.

• To heal, parents need to actively remember the child who died and commemorate the life that was lived.

• Never let anyone take your memories away in a misguided attempt to save you from pain. It's good for you to continue to display photos of your child. It's good to talk about memories, both happy and sad. It's good to cherish clothing and other items that belonged to your child.

• In the early weeks and months of your grief, you may fear that you will forget your child—the details of her face, the tone of his voice, the special lilt in her walk. Rest assured that while time may blur some of your memories, as you slowly shift your relationship from one of presence to one of memory, you will indeed remember.

• Remembering the past makes hoping for the future possible.

CARPE DIEM:
You might find it helpful to begin to write down memories of your child. This is both a healing exercise and a way to hold onto special memories forever. Today, write down at least one memory.

11.

UNDERSTAND THE SIX NEEDS OF MOURNING

Need #4: Develop a new self-identity

• A big part of your self-identity was formed by the relationship you had with the child who died.

• You have gone from being a parent to a "bereaved parent." You thought of yourself, at least in part, as your child's mother or father. Even if you have other children, this perception of yourself has changed. If the child who died was your only child, you may wonder whether you are still a parent at all.

• While you must work through this difficult need yourself, I can assure you that you are and always will be your child's parent, for to parent is to walk through a door that can never be closed.

• Still, the way you defined yourself and the way society defines you is changed. You need to re-anchor yourself, to reconstruct your self-identity. This is arduous and painful work.

CARPE DIEM:
Write out a response to this prompt: I used to be
_____. Now that _____ died, I am
_____. This makes me feel _____.
Keep writing as long as you want.

12.

UNDERSTAND THE SIX
NEEDS OF MOURNING

Need #5: Search for meaning.

• When someone loved dies, we naturally question the meaning and purpose of life and death. When a child dies before a parent, these kinds of questions are particularly painful. Why should a child die before his mother and father? This death violates nature and the order of the universe. Your child gave your life meaning and purpose.

• "Why?" questions may surface uncontrollably and often precede "How?" questions. "Why did this happen?" comes before "How will I go on living?"

• You will almost certainly question your philosophy of life and explore religious and spiritual values as you work on this need.

• Remember that having faith or spirituality does not negate your need to mourn. If you believe in an afterlife of some kind, both you and your child have still lost precious time on Earth. It's normal to feel dumbfounded and angry at a God whom you may feel has permitted such a thing to happen.

• Ultimately, you may decide that there is no answer to the question "Why did this happen?" The death does not make sense. It never will.

CARPE DIEM:

Write down a list of "why" questions that have surfaced for you since the death. Find a friend or counselor who will explore these questions with you without thinking she has to give you answers.

13.

UNDERSTAND THE SIX NEEDS OF MOURNING

Need #6: Receive ongoing support from others.

- As mourners, we need the love and understanding of others if we are to heal.

- Don't feel ashamed by your heightened dependence on others right now. If the death was recent, you may feel the need to be around people all the time. You may need to talk about the death often. You may need help getting meals together, doing laundry, completing paperwork. Don't feel bad about this. Instead, take comfort in the knowledge that others care about you.

- Unfortunately, our society places too much value on "carrying on" and "doing well" after a death. So, many mourners are abandoned by their friends and family soon after the death. If the death of your child was long ago, you may have experienced this abandonment firsthand. Keep in mind the rule of thirds: one-third of your friends will be supportive of your need to mourn, one-third will make you feel worse, and one-third will neither help nor hinder.

- Grief is experienced in "doses" over years, not quickly and efficiently, and you will need the continued support of your friends and family for weeks, months and years. If you are not getting this support, ask for it. Usually people are more than willing to help— they just don't have any idea what to do (and what not to do).

CARPE DIEM:

Sometimes your friends want to support you but don't know how. Ask. Call your closest friend right now and tell him you need his help through the coming weeks and months. Even if the death was years ago, renewing the subject with a close friend will help him understand that your grief is still very much a part of your life.

14.

KNOW THAT GRIEF DOES NOT PROCEED IN ORDERLY, PREDICTABLE "STAGES."

- Though the "Needs of Mourning" (Ideas 8-13) are numbered 1-6, grief is not an orderly progression towards healing. Don't fall into the trap of thinking your grief journey will be predictable or always forward-moving. Mourning is really a "dosed" process of readapting to life with loss and continues throughout our lives.

- Usually, grief hurts more before it hurts less.

- You will probably experience a multitude of different emotions in a wave-like fashion. You will also likely encounter more than one need of mourning at the same time.

- Be compassionate with yourself as you experience your own unique grief journey.

CARPE DIEM:
Has anyone told you that you are in this or that "stage" of grief? Ignore this usually well-intentioned advice. Don't allow yourself or anyone else to compartmentalize your grief.

15.

CRY.

- Tears are a natural cleansing and healing mechanism. It's OK to cry. In fact, it's good to cry when you feel like it. What's more, tears are a form of mourning. They are sacred!

- On the other hand, don't feel bad if you aren't crying a lot. Not everyone is a crier. Some fathers, in particular, do not feel the need to cry, especially as the death grows more distant. The inability to cry is not necessarily a deficit.

- You may find that those around you are uncomfortable with your tears. As a society, we're often not so good at witnessing others in pain.

- Explain to your friends and family that you need to cry right now and that they can help by allowing you to.

- You may find yourself crying at unexpected times or places. If you need to, excuse yourself and retreat to somewhere private.

CARPE DIEM:

If you feel like it, have a good cry today. Find a safe place to embrace your pain and cry as long and as hard as you want to.

16.

BE AWARE THAT YOUR GRIEF AFFECTS YOUR BODY, HEART, SOCIAL SELF AND SPIRIT.

- Grief is physically demanding. The body responds to the stress of the encounter and the immune system can weaken. You may be more susceptible to illness and physical discomforts. Grieving parents often describe their grief as a pain in the chest or a physical ache. You will probably also feel sluggish or highly fatigued. Some people call this the "lethargy of grief."

- The emotional toll of grief is complex and painful. Mourners often feel many different feelings, and those feelings can shift and blur over time.

- Bereavement naturally results in social discomfort. Friends and family often withdraw from mourners, leaving us isolated and unsupported. Mourners often feel out of place in a setting they once felt a part of.

- Mourners often ask, "Why go on living?" "Will my life have meaning now?" "Where is God in this?" Spiritual questions such as these are natural and necessary but also draining.

- All four facets of your self are under attack. You may feel weak and powerless, especially in the early weeks and months. Only over time will you gain the strength to fight back.

CARPE DIEM:
If you've felt physically affected by your grief, see a doctor this week. Sometimes it's comforting to receive a clean bill of health.

17.

EXPECT TO HAVE A MULTITUDE OF FEELINGS.

- Grieving parents don't just feel sad. They often feel numb, angry, guilty, afraid, regretful, confused, even relieved (in cases of chronic or terminal illness, for example). Sometimes these feelings follow each other within a short period of time or they may occur simultaneously. I often say that grief is not experienced as a single note but as a chord.

- As strange as some of these emotions may seem to you, they are normal and healthy. At times, you may feel like you're "going crazy." Rest assured that you aren't going crazy, you're grieving.

- Allow yourself to feel whatever it is you are feeling without judging yourself.

- Talk about your feelings with someone who cares and can supportively listen.

CARPE DIEM:
Which grief feeling has surprised you most? Make a point of talking about this feeling with someone today.

18.

KNOW THAT IT'S OK TO FEEL ANGRY.

- Grieving parents often feel angry—at others whom they perceive caused or contributed to the death, at themselves for letting it happen, at God, even at the child herself for having abandoned them.

- Anger is a normal and necessary way to protest the death. It's a way of lashing out against the universe and sometimes fixing blame. It's a way of dealing with feelings of fear and powerlessness.

- It's OK to feel angry. What you do with your anger, however, makes all the difference. Express it in appropriate ways without hurting yourself or others. Let it out or it will fester inside you.

- It's also perfectly OK not to feel angry. Watch out for well-intentioned people who may prescribe that you should feel angry. Feel what you feel.

CARPE DIEM:

Whom are you angry with about the death? Write a letter to this person expressing all your thoughts and feelings, but don't mail it. Sit on the letter for a month or two then read it again or show it to someone else. There are some instances in which it may be appropriate to mail the letter, but in most situations face-to-face communication may be preferable.

19.

FIND WAYS TO UNDERSTAND AND COME TO THE LIMITS OF YOUR GUILT.

- I've learned that many grieving parents feel guilty about one thing or another. They feel guilty that they didn't stop their child from driving that night, that they didn't take their child to the doctor sooner, that they weren't perfect parents, that somehow their child ended up paying the ultimate price for their own sins.

- You loved your child. You were a good parent. You were not a perfect parent, but no one is. Do you believe that you were responsible for your child's conception and birth? Or was some greater power responsible for that miracle? Perhaps the death was equally in the hands of a greater power.

- Talk about any lingering feelings of guilt, regret and remorse. Don't nurse them and continue to punish yourself for them. Instead, give them voice and see how their power over you diminishes.

- Rationally or irrationally, some grieving parents blame their spouses for some aspect of the death. If feelings of blame reside in you, talk compassionately (remember, his or her heart is also broken) to your spouse about them and see a counselor together.

- I would be remiss if I did not point out that some parents are in fact partly or wholly responsible for their child's death, whether it was intentional or accidental. These parents often benefit from professional help in dealing with their overwhelming guilt.

CARPE DIEM:
Call a friend who's a good listener or sit down with your partner and say, "I need to tell someone about..." Get any feelings of guilt, remorse and regret off your chest.

20.

MOVE TOWARD YOUR GRIEF, NOT AWAY FROM IT.

- Our society teaches us that emotional pain is to be avoided, not embraced, yet it is only in moving toward our grief that we can be healed.

- As previously noted, the only way to get to the other side is through.

- Be suspicious if you find yourself thinking that you're "doing well" since the death. Sometimes "doing well" means you're avoiding your pain or you're simply experiencing the natural numbness of grief.

- Of course, it's also necessary to dose yourself with your grief. Sometimes you will need to distract yourself from the pain. But in general, you should feel that you're moving toward your grief— toward an understanding and acceptance of it.

CARPE DIEM:

Today, talk to someone else who loved your child. Share your thoughts and feelings with him openly and encourage him to do the same. Support each other in your grief.

21.

PREPARE TO ANSWER "THE QUESTION."

- "How many children do you have?" What was once an everyday, friendly question is now a loaded gun.

- How will you answer ? If you had three children and one dies, do you say you have two children? If you had a single child and he dies, do you say you have no children? To many grieving parents, leaving out the child who has died seems like disloyalty or worse yet, like an erasure of the child's entire existence. Yet including the child who has died and then having to explain the death is a sure way to bog down an otherwise casual conversation.

- Most grieving parents come up with standard answers to "The Question," though their responses vary depending on whom they are talking to and in what situation. Here are a few of their ideas:
  - "I have two surviving children. Mary is 10 and Alex is 3."
  - Simply: "Yes, I have children. Let me show you a picture. Mary is 10 and Alex is 3."
  - If you believe in heaven, you might say, "I have two children here on earth and one waiting for me in heaven."
  - If you had two children and one died: "I have two children. One is alive and one has died."
  - If your only child died: "Yes, one son (or one daughter)." If the questions persist: "Jeff died when he was 16. That was 3 years ago."

- I'm told that answering "The Question" gets easier and more natural over time. You will discover how you are most comfortable answering this question.

CARPE DIEM:
Talk with your spouse or a friend about how to handle "The Question" so you won't be so caught off-guard when the next person asks you.

22.

COMMUNICATE OPENLY WITH YOUR FAMILY.

- Your partner and your surviving children are hurting, too—each in their own unique ways. Nobody can (or should try to) take away the hurt, but talking about all your thoughts and feelings since the death helps everybody feel supported and understood.

- Is yours an "open family system," in which members openly talk about the death, the person who died and their grief? Or is yours a "closed family system," in which members pretty much keep their thoughts and feelings to themselves and don't feel safe mourning among their own family?

- Grief is hard enough without losing the support of those we love most. And even though your parental grief is especially difficult, keep in mind that how you're expressing your own grief affects how others in your family will. If you're able to express your grief openly, you will be a positive model, allowing others to express theirs as well, particularly your surviving children.

- It's never too late to communicate openly with your family. Even if up until now yours has been a "closed family system," you can open it up by starting to talk, little by little, day by day, about the child who died and the death. Such discussions may be painful at first, but I promise you that over time, everyone's grief journeys will be eased tremendously.

CARPE DIEM:

Today, mention the child who died to your spouse or a surviving child. Share a memory or bring up a regret. Ask how the other person is feeling about the loss.

23.

USE THE NAME OF YOUR CHILD.

- When you're talking about the death or about your life in general, don't avoid using the name of the child who has died. Sometimes others are afraid to use the name in your presence out of fear that it is painful to you. If you use the name, others will know that they can use it, too.

- Acknowledge the significance of the death by talking about your child: "I remember when David . . .," "I was thinking of Sarah today because . . .," "Jordan always loved your pecan pie . . ."

- Ask your friends and family to use your child's name, too. Grieving parents often love to hear that special name.

CARPE DIEM:

Flip through a baby name book at a local bookstore or library and look up the name of your child. Reflect on the name's meaning as it relates to the unique person you loved.

24.

TELL THE STORY, OVER AND OVER AGAIN IF YOU FEEL THE NEED.

- Acknowledging a death is a painful, ongoing task that we accomplish in doses, over time. A vital part of healing in grief is often "telling the story" over and over again. It's as if each time you tell the story, it becomes a little more real.

- The "story" relates the circumstances surrounding the death of the child, reviewing the relationship you had with the child, describing aspects of the personality of the child who died, and sharing memories, good and bad.

- Grieving parents can almost always recount in vivid and very specific detail what the day of the death was like for them.

- Find people who are willing to listen to you tell your story, over and over again if necessary, without judgment.

- You and your spouse may find great comfort in telling each other stories and sharing memories of the child's life. Ask your spouse to tell you the story of the time when . . .

CARPE DIEM:
Tell the story to someone today in the form of a letter. Perhaps you can write and send this letter to a friend who lives far away.

25.

REACH OUT AND TOUCH.

- For many people, physical contact with another human being is healing. It has been recognized since ancient times as having transformative, healing powers. Touch often replaces words when words are inadequate.

- Have you hugged anyone lately? Held someone's hand? Put your arm around another human being?

- You probably know several people who enjoy hugging or physical touching. If you're comfortable with their touch, encourage it in the weeks and months to come.

- Hug someone you feel safe with. Kiss your surviving children or a friend's baby. Walk arm in arm with a neighbor.

- Getting a massage is another way of receiving healing touch. Schedule an appointment for a full body massage today, or, if this makes you uncomfortable, a shoulder and neck massage might work wonders.

CARPE DIEM:

Try hugging a close friend or family member today, even if you usually don't. You might be surprised at the comfort it brings.

26.

TREASURE YOUR CONCEPT OF WHO YOUR CHILD WAS.

- Your child was smart, funny, handsome, sweet. Despite his flaws, you loved him unconditionally.

- After his death, you may find that others beg to differ about your child's characteristics or personality. Some may tell you stories about his misbehavior, for example, or less-than-desirable qualities in an attempt to knock him down a peg or two. It's as if they think that rendering him less perfect will ease your grief. Your surviving children may also feel they can never live up to your image of the child who died.

- Allow yourself to cling to those things you loved best about your child. Over time, you may find that discussing all aspects of his character or personality—good and bad—with others who knew him will help you work through conflicting thoughts and feelings.

- A caution: Try not to compare your surviving children to the child who died. I've learned that surviving children often feel they can't possibly live up to the parent's ideal of the dead child. Other times surviving siblings will conceal the fact that they are trying to be "both children" for you. Your surviving children need to feel loved, respected and valued for who they are.

CARPE DIEM:

Gather special photos of the child who died and place them in a small photo album—one you can keep in your purse or your desk drawer. Try to select photos that capture well your child's personality, character and passions.

27.

KNOW THAT YOU ARE LOVED.

- Love gives our lives meaning. To heal, you must learn to love fully again.

- But you are also an object of the affection of others. There are people who love you. There are people who want you to be happy again.

- Those who love you may not know how to reach out to you in grief, but they still love you. Even in their silence, people are doing the best they can with your loss.

- Think about the people who care about you and the ways in which your life matters.

CARPE DIEM:
Spend some time today with someone who loves you.
Focus on this person and what she is saying. Tell
her how much you love her, too.

28.

WORK ON YOUR MARRIAGE.

- Some say that divorce is prevalent among grieving parents, but in my experience it is no more common among grieving parents than among other married couples. About half of all marriages in the U.S. end in divorce anyway. It could well be that grieving parents who divorce were bound to get divorced in the first place. Watch out for people who proclaim, "I heard if your child dies you end up getting divorced."

- Do not think of the death of your child as a fatal blow to your marriage and it probably won't be. If you loved your spouse before the death and intended to stay married forever, there is no reason your marriage cannot continue to succeed. Yes, there will be additional stress, and your marriage may need more open communication and nourishing in the months and years following the death. But it is not doomed to fail.

- Grief is primarily a journey of the self. You and your spouse cannot grieve "together" or even in the same ways. But you can be there for each other, talk and listen, accept differences, honor feelings, bear witness. And you can and should work on your marriage. As one parent told me, "We walked on different pathways, but we tried to hold hands as we did."

- Working on your marriage means continuing to communicate about all that goes on in life. The death of your child is just one part of this. It also means spending time together, both in work and in play. It means sharing dreams and joys, failures and sorrows.

- "At least you have each other," people may say to you. At first, this may not feel like a blessing because you're both so overcome by your own unique grief. But over time, your redefined love for each other as well as your shared history may indeed strengthen the bonds of marriage.

CARPE DIEM:
Make a date with your spouse. Surprise him or her with a special evening together, whether out on the town or at home.

29.

COMMUNICATE WITH YOUR PARTNER ABOUT YOUR SEX LIFE.

- Grieving parents often struggle with how and when to continue their sex lives. Certainly not always, but often, grieving wives are slower to feel ready to embrace pleasure while grieving husbands crave the intimacy, pleasure and escape.

- Both feelings are understandable and normal. And there is no one right way to handle this problem; there is only communicating about it.

- If your partner wants sex and you don't, say why. Be honest.

- Don't force your partner into anything he or she's not ready for. Insisting will only breed resentment later on.

- Be prepared for lovemaking with your spouse to be more emotional in the early weeks and months after the death.

- Eventually, most couples settle back into a normal sexual pattern. If you don't see this happening in your marriage or are unhappy with your sex life, seeing a marriage counselor may be an effective way to air concerns and rekindle intimacies.

CARPE DIEM:

Initiate a frank discussion about sex with your partner today.
Discuss your feelings and needs and hopes for the future.

30.

ALLOW YOURSELF TO FEEL SELFISH OR RESENTFUL.

- Many grieving parents have taught me that they feel resentment towards others, particularly in the early days and weeks after the death. Condolence cards and phone calls pour in, friends and neighbors visit, memorial contributions are made, yet the grieving parent may be thinking, "You tell me you're sorry, but you have no #*&%#! idea."

- It's normal to feel resentment towards others untouched by the death of a child. Their children are alive and well, their family is intact, what do they know about hardship? Why you and not them?

- Selfish feelings help you survive. Your self has been assaulted and you need to focus on tending to the wounds right now. Over time, these feelings will dissipate and you will better appreciate the supportive words and actions of others.

- Enlist the help of someone outside your immediate family to keep track of phone calls, condolence cards, flowers and memorial contributions. This person can be responsible for sending thank you notes and following up. Months and years from now, you may take comfort in reading the cards and remembering the support.

CARPE DIEM:

If the death was recent, ask a close friend to serve as a buffer between you and the world. If the death was longer ago and you feel ready, phone or write a note to someone thanking him for his kind words or deeds at the time of the death.

31.

GET AWAY FROM IT ALL.

- Sometimes it takes a change of scenery to reveal the texture of our lives.

- New people and places help us see our lives from a new vantage point and can assist us in our search for meaning.

- Often, getting away from it all means leaving civilization behind and retreating to nature. But it can also mean temporarily abandoning your environment and spending time in one that's altogether different.

- Visit a foreign country. Go backpacking in the wilderness. Volunteer in the inner city. Spend a weekend at a monastery or nunnery.

- However, temper your enthusiasm with realistic expectations. Sometimes "getting away from it all" is not as transformative an experience as we had hoped.

CARPE DIEM:
Plan a trip to somewhere far away. Ask a friend to travel with you.

32.

SAY NO.

- Especially soon after your child's death, you may lack the energy as well as the desire to participate in activities you used to find pleasurable.

- It's OK to say no when you're asked to help with a project or attend a party. Learn how to do it politely but firmly. Say, without apologizing too profusely, "No, I can't right now. But thanks for thinking of me."

- If you communicate better in writing, write a note to the people who've invited you and explain your feelings. Be sure to thank them for the invitation.

- Realize that you can't keep saying no forever. There will always be that first wedding, christening, birthday party, etc. Don't miss out on life's most joyful celebrations. If you attend something and find it overwhelming, it's OK to excuse yourself and leave early.

CARPE DIEM:
Say no to something today. Allow yourself not to feel guilty about it.

33.

PRACTICE BREATHING IN AND OUT.

- Sometimes what we need most is just to "be." In our goal-oriented society, many of us have lost the knack for simply living.

- Besides, just "being" may be all you feel up to right now. And that's OK.

- Drop all your plans and obligations for today and do nothing.

- Meditate if meditation helps center you. Find someplace quiet, be still, close your eyes and focus on breathing in and out. Relax your muscles. Listen to your own heartbeat.

CARPE DIEM:
Sit down, focus on something 20-30 feet
away and take 10 deep breaths.

34.

RESET YOUR CLOCK.

- When a child dies, there is only Before and After. There is your life Before the death and now there is your life After the death. It's as if your internal calendar gets reset to mark the significance of the profound loss.

- Many grieving parents can tell you, without thought or conscious calculation, how many years, months and days it has been since their child died.

- These new ways of keeping time are perfectly normal. You are not crazy! Your mind and heart have simply come up with a new system to mark the earth's relentless rotation.

- It's also OK to mention your new timekeeping system in everyday conversation: "Thanksgiving's coming. My son died four Thanksgivings ago." Comments such as these let others know that it's important to you to remember and to continue to tell the story.

CARPE DIEM:

Write two columns on a piece of paper: Before and After. In ten minutes, brainstorm as many adjectives or feelings that you can think of that define each time period.

35.

TAKE SOME TIME OFF WORK.

- Typically, our society grants us three days "bereavement leave" and then expects us to return to work as if nothing happened. Grieving parents are often given a little more latitude, but you may still feel like you can't possibly function at work in the weeks and months after the death.

- Even if the death was long ago, you may want to take some time off work to complete a project, to travel, or to reassess your life.

- Some companies will grant extended leaves of absence or sabbaticals in some situations.

- If you simply can't take off additional time, request that your work load be lightened for the next several months. Ask to work a four-day work week.

CARPE DIEM:
Take a spiritual day off today. Spend the day
resting or doing something restorative.

36.

GO EASY ON PEOPLE WHO SAY STUPID THINGS.

- I'm sure you've realized by now that people don't know what to say to a grieving parent. Often they say the wrong things:
  - "Time heals all wounds."
  - "God wouldn't give you more than you can handle."
  - "At least you had her as long as you did."
  - "You can have another child."
  - "Now you have an angel in heaven."
  - "You'll grow so much stronger because of this."
  - "I know how you feel."

- Most of these people are well-intentioned. They truly don't realize how phrases like these diminish your unique and significant loss. Perhaps instead of getting angry at them, you can keep in mind that they are, in fact, trying to help. How many hurtful things did you inadvertently say to mourners before your loss? As Maya Angelou wrote, "You did what you knew how to do and when you knew better, you did better."

- Sometimes entering into an honest, deeper discussion with such people about what the death has really been like for you is a way to break through the clichés, helping them as well as you.

CARPE DIEM:

Try talking with your partner (or a close friend) about the hurtful remarks others sometimes make. Say, "Don't you hate it when people say..." This conversation may help you express your feelings of hurt and frustration.

37.

BE COMPASSIONATE IN JUDGING OTHER PARENTS.

- Even for the most loving, level-headed, patient, giving parents, raising children is hard. It's unending work, day in and day out. It's tiring, trying, exasperating.

- Yet you now know, with the benefit of 20/20 hindsight, that all the bad that comes with raising children does not equal even one single speck in the universe of the good. Children are indeed our greatest gifts.

- If you're like many grieving parents, you get annoyed when other parents complain about the challenges of daily life. You are stunned when parents ignore their children or hurt them. You want to shake them and scream, "Love your child! She may not be here tomorrow!"

- For the most part, it's best to keep your judgments to yourself. Just as you did before your child's death, most parents are doing the best they can. That's not to say that you shouldn't offer a little perspective now and then. A few choice, gentle words from you just might help another parent see the tiniest glimpse of what you see.

CARPE DIEM:
If you think it's appropriate, write a note to a parent who is struggling and needs a few words of encouragement. Tell her, gently and nonjudgmentally, what the death of your child has taught you about what's truly important.

38.

UNDERSTAND THE UNIQUE NEEDS OF GRIEVING FATHERS.

- While grieving mothers tend to mourn more openly, some grieving fathers tend to be more stoic and quicker to return to work and daily routines. I believe this is because society has trained and expects men to act this way—not because they're naturally unfeeling. On the other hand, I have also seen these typical gender roles reversed, with the father being the more emotional, expressive partner.

- Grieving fathers are often "forgotten mourners" because family and friends tend to focus their support on grieving mothers. If they are the main breadwinners in the family, fathers are often expected to return to work a few days after the death. A sense of being defined by their careers also contributes to their early return to work.

- So, grieving fathers often keep a stiff upper lip and seem, on the outside, to be "doing well." Actually, they're often slowly drowning in their own despair, sinking into depression while nobody seems to notice.

- Moreover, masculine ways of grieving are often inherently different. Grieving fathers may focus more on preventing other deaths, seeking justice, actively "doing something" about the death. They may feel an intense desire to protect their remaining family (and a sense of failure at having not protected the child who died). They truly may not feel the need to cry. All these responses are normal and natural as long as the grieving father is finding ways to express his feelings.

- If you're a grieving father, seek the help of others. Talk about your grief and the child who died. Take some time off work if you can. Be open with your spouse and your surviving children.

CARPE DIEM:

If you're a grieving father, make a point of mourning in some way today. Express or talk about your grief in a way that feels right for you.

39.

UNDERSTAND THE UNIQUE NEEDS OF GRIEVING MOTHERS.

- The mother-child bond is usually profoundly strong. Mothers seem to be wired to take care of their children and tend to their every need.

- Moreover, women are often defined as mothers, first and foremost, by themselves and by society—even if they are independent, well-rounded, career-minded individuals.

- Women are also generally more emotional, more able to express their feelings and seek and accept the support of others. (Though sometimes, as I have mentioned, the father is more open and emotional.)

- So, grieving mothers tend to grieve intensely longer. They are often unable to return to daily routines for weeks or months. They tend to cry more openly. And they often feel resentment at their husbands for not seeming to feel or act as they do.

- Sometimes grieving mothers need to know it's OK not to focus on the death and their grief to the exclusion of everything else. They need support in seeking pleasure and taking care of themselves. They need permission to be selfish. They need permission to work outside of the home if they want to, perhaps part-time.

CARPE DIEM:
If you're a grieving mother, consider your life
outside your family. Who are you? What gives you joy?
What can you do for yourself today?

40.

UNDERSTAND THE UNIQUE NEEDS OF GRIEVING GRANDPARENTS.

- Your parents and your spouse's parents, like grieving siblings and sometimes grieving fathers, can be "forgotten mourners." Ongoing support and consideration are often not paid to grieving grandparents.

- When a grandchild dies, the grandparent often mourns the death on many levels. The grandparent probably loved the child dearly and may have been very close to her. The death has created a hole in the grandparent's life that cannot be filled by anyone else. Grandparents who were not close to the child who died, perhaps because they lived far away, may instead mourn the loss of a relationship they never had.

- Grieving grandparents are also faced with witnessing their child— you or your spouse—mourn the death. A parent's love for a child is perhaps the strongest of all human bonds. For you, the pain of grief may seem intolerable. For the grandparents, watching you suffer so and feeling powerless to take away the hurt can feel almost as intolerable.

- For grandparents, who may have lived long, rich lives already, the struggle to understand the death may bring about feelings of guilt. "Why didn't God take me, instead?" the grandparent may ask. "Why couldn't it have been me?"

- Unfortunately, some grandparents may not be able to talk openly with you about their pain and you may feel shut out. This is sometimes a generational issue and is their way of coping.

CARPE DIEM:

If you haven't done so lately, talk to your parents and/or your in-laws about your child. Ask them what they miss most about the child who died or what they remember best about him.

41.

WEAR A SYMBOL OF MOURNING.

- In centuries past, grieving mothers often made jewelry or wreaths out of locks of hair that belonged to the child who died. Black clothing was required for a period of one year. Mourners wore black armbands.

- These symbols of mourning accorded a special status to mourners, saying, in effect, "Someone I love has died. Please offer me your respect and your condolences."

- Today, we no longer identify mourners in these ways, creating the harmful illusion that "everything's back to normal" even though it's not (and never will be).

- How do you let others know that you're still in mourning and still need their support? The best way is to tell them. Talk about the death and its continuing impact on your life. Let your friends and family know you still need their help.

CARPE DIEM:

Make a symbol of mourning part of your everyday dress. Some parents wear jewelry that belonged to the child who died. You might fill a locket with a photo and a lock of hair or wear a photo button on your jacket. Or sew a black armband and wear it proudly.

42.

VISIT THE CEMETERY.

- Visiting the cemetery or the place in which the remains were scattered is an important mourning ritual for many grieving parents. It helps them embrace their loss and remember their child.

- Some grieving parents spend time at the gravesite every week. Some visit on holidays, birthdays and anniversaries.

- Still others find no solace or meaning in visiting the cemetery. "That's not where my child is. He's in heaven!" one mother told me. If the cemetery isn't for you, that's fine, as long as you're not simply avoiding all reminders of your child's death.

- Ask a friend or family member to go with you. You may feel comforted by their presence. Some parents have taught me that they prefer to go to the cemetery by themselves and that they find this a very spiritual time.

- Don't force others to visit the cemetery with you. Some grieving siblings have told me that they were forced to visit the cemetery and resented every minute of it. If your surviving children don't find visits to the cemetery healing, find other ways to mourn as a family.

CARPE DIEM:

If you can, drop by the cemetery with a picnic lunch of foods that your child loved best. Share the lunch with your spouse or a friend or munch on it yourself while you think about your child.

43.

FIND WAYS TO CONTINUE YOUR RELATIONSHIP WITH THE CHILD WHO DIED.

- When a child dies, do you still have a relationship with her? Yes, you have a relationship of memory. Spend time nurturing your memories. When you feel up to it, tell stories, look through photos, watch videotapes, ask others to tell you stories about the child.

- There are also ways to make the child part of your current life. Some grieving parents regularly "talk" to the child's photo, updating her on what's going on, sharing little things and big things. Some grieving parents make visits to the cemetery a part of each week. Some "talk" to their children each night, silently communicating with the child they believe still exists in another dimension.

- Still other grieving parents embrace their child's hopes and dreams and make carrying those hopes and dreams forward for others part of their ongoing lives. They in effect take on a mission as a way of continuing their relationship with and honoring the child who died.

- All of these practices are normal and healthy, and you'll probably find them to be comforting, too.

CARPE DIEM:
Have you tried any of the above ways of continuing your relationship with your child? If not, maybe you want to give one a try today and see how it feels for you.

44.

UNDERSTAND THE ROLE
OF "LINKING OBJECTS."

- Grieving parents are often comforted by physical objects associated with the child who died. It is not unusual to save clothing, jewelry, toys, locks of hair and other personal items. (Also see Idea 45 on what to do with your child's bedroom.)

- Such "linking objects" will help you remember your child and honor the life that was lived. Such objects may help you heal.

- Never think that being attached to these objects is morbid or wrong. If someone tells you that you're crazy for wearing your son's sweatshirt or not washing your daughter's pillowcase, ignore them. You're not crazy; you're simply holding on to what you have left.

- Never hurry into disposing of your child's belongings. You may want to leave personal items untouched for months or sometimes years. This is OK as long as the objects offer comfort and don't inhibit healing.

CARPE DIEM:
When and only when you're ready, ask a friend or family member to help you sort through your child's belongings. Fill a memory box with significant objects and mementos.

45.

DO WHAT FEELS RIGHT WITH YOUR CHILD'S ROOM AND BELONGINGS.

- Knowing what to do with their child's belongings—and when to do it—seems to be a particularly difficult decision for grieving parents.

- As with all things in grief, there is no one right way to handle this issue. You must do what feels right for you and your family.

- Many grieving parents keep their child's room just as it was when the child died, in effect creating a sort of shrine. Actually, I like to call it a temple, not a shrine. While some would argue with me, I think this practice is fine—for a time. In the early months and years after the death, you may need the room as a mourning retreat, a sacred space in which to remember and mourn for your child. Over time, however, it's probably better to convert the room to a different use. And remember—doing what's right for you AND your family means considering the emotional environment of the household and taking into consideration what others in your household would like to do with the room.

- When you're ready to sort through your child's belongings (and do go slowly; there are no rewards for speed!), consider which items might be meaningful to others who loved your child. A friend might like that CD, a grandparent might appreciate a piece of artwork, a teacher might like a photo. This will help them feel and be forevermore connected to your child.

- Do keep at least a box of special items just for yourself.

CARPE DIEM:
Bring some of the smaller special items that belonged to your child into a frame shop and ask for help in creating a special shadow box.

46.

LET GO OF DESTRUCTIVE MYTHS ABOUT GRIEF AND MOURNING.

- You have probably internalized many of our society's harmful myths about grief and mourning.

- Here are some to let go of:
  - I need to be strong and carry on.
  - I need to get ahold of myself!
  - Tears are a sign of weakness.
  - I need to get over my grief.
  - Death is something we don't talk about.
  - My child wouldn't want me to be sad.

- Sometimes these myths will cause you to feel guilty about or ashamed of your true thoughts and feelings.

- Your grief is your grief. It's normal and necessary. Allow it to be what it is.

CARPE DIEM:
Which grief myth have you encountered most since the death?
Write about it in your journal.

47.

LIVE FOR YOUR CHILD.

- Grieving parents have taught me that one important way they go on not just living but living well is by living on behalf of their child. Their child's precious life has been taken. This makes it especially important that they do not squander their own.

- Death often leaves grieving parents feeling powerless. You were powerless to prevent the death and you're powerless to reverse it. But you can regain a feeling of power by deciding to take control of the rest of your life.

- Lots of grieving parents take up a new life direction after the death of a child, and often that new direction comes in part from the child's own hopes and dreams. If a son wanted to be a concert pianist, for example, the parents might devote a lot of time to helping other young piano players receive the proper training, instruments and opportunities.

- What did your child love in life? How can you help nurture that love in the world in an ongoing, positive way?

- Sometimes living for your child simply means living mindfully, with an appreciation for all that is good and beautiful and with a deep, abiding kindness to others.

CARPE DIEM:
What did your child love in life? Find a way to honor that love today.

48.

KNOW THAT IT'S NORMAL TO RETHINK DEATH.

- Many grieving parents have taught me that the death of a child changes the ways in which they think about their own deaths. Most grieving parents do not fear death. While they do not have a "death wish," some actually look forward to dying because they are hopeful they will be reunited with their child.

- Grieving parents also often think differently about subsequent deaths in the family. They sometimes feel comforted by the fact that the person who has just died has gone to be with their child.

- Passing thoughts of suicide are also normal. Many grieving parents say that they "want to die" in the early days after the death. This feeling usually wanes after a few weeks or months. If you have suicidal thoughts that do not subside or that seem very intense, please get professional help immediately.

CARPE DIEM:
Consider how you used to feel about death and how you feel about it now. How can you leverage this difference to improve the quality of your life?

49.

WRITE A LETTER.

- Sometimes articulating our thoughts and feelings in letter-form helps us understand them better.

- Write a letter or a birthday card to your child telling him how you feel now that he's gone. Consider the following prompts:
  - What I miss most about you is . . .
  - What I wish I'd said or hadn't said is . . .
  - What's hardest for me now is . . .
  - What I'd like to ask you is . . .
  - When you were born . . .
  - I'm keeping my memories of you alive by . . .

- Consider reading your letter aloud at the cemetery. Or ask your spouse to read it.

- Write a letter to God telling him how you feel about the death.

- Write thank you notes to helpers such as hospice staff, neighbors, doctors, funeral directors, etc.

CARPE DIEM:
Write a letter to someone you love who's still alive,
perhaps a surviving child or a close friend, telling
him why he's so very important to you.

50.

DON'T EXPECT YOURSELF TO MOURN OR HEAL IN A CERTAIN WAY OR IN A CERTAIN TIME.

- Your unique grief journey will be shaped by many factors, including:
  - the nature of the relationship you had with your child.
  - the age of your child.
  - the circumstances of the death.
  - your unique personality.
  - your cultural background.
  - your religious or spiritual beliefs.
  - your gender.
  - your support systems.

- Because of these and other factors, no two deaths are ever mourned in precisely the same way.

- Don't have rigid expectations for your thoughts, feelings and behaviors.

CARPE DIEM:
Draw two columns on a piece of paper. Title the left column "What I used to think grief would be like." Title the right column "What it's really like." Jot down notes in both columns.

51.

BE MINDFUL OF ANNIVERSARIES.

- Anniversaries—of the death, life events, birthdays—are typically difficult for grieving parents. Days that used to so very special are now painful reminders of what has been lost.

- These are times you may want to plan ahead for. Perhaps you could take a day off work on the anniversary of the death. Maybe on your child's next birthday you could visit the cemetery or plan a small family gathering.

- Don't expect family and friends to always remember these important days. Instead, be proactive and reach out to them. Make plans. Talk about your feelings with a close friend.

- For some grieving parents, the anticipation of the anniversary or the days immediately following the anniversary are more difficult than the anniversary day itself.

CARPE DIEM:
What's the next anniversary you've been dreading? Make
a plan right now for what you will do on that day. Enlist
a friend's help so you won't be alone.

52.

TAKE GOOD CARE OF YOURSELF.

- Good self-care is nurturing and necessary for mourners, yet it's something many of us completely overlook.

- Try very hard to eat well and get adequate rest. Lay your body down 2-3 times a day for 20-30 minutes, even if you don't sleep. I know—you probably don't care very much about eating well right now, and you may be sleeping poorly. But taking care of yourself is truly one way to fuel healing and to begin to embrace life again.

- Drink at least 5-6 glasses of water each day. Dehydration can compound feelings of fatigue and disorientation.

- Exercise not only provides you with more energy, it can give you focused thinking time. Take a 20-minute walk every day. Or, if that seems too much, a five-minute walk. But don't over-exercise, because your body needs extra rest, as well.

- Now more than ever, you need to allow time for you.

CARPE DIEM:
Are you taking a multi-vitamin? If not, now
is probably a good time to start.

53.

KEEP A JOURNAL.

- Journals are an ideal way for some mourners to record thoughts and feelings.

- Remember—your inner thoughts and feelings of grief need to be expressed outwardly (which includes writing) if you are to heal.

- Consider jotting down your thoughts and feelings each night before you go to sleep. Your journal entries can be as long or as short as you want.

- One way to keep a grief journal is to write to the child who died. Tell her about your day. Tell her how much you miss her. Tell her what you're struggling with most.

- Or keep a dream journal, instead. Keep a blank book in your nightstand for recording your dreams when you wake up.

- If you're not a writer, that's OK, too. Some people are journalers and some are not.

CARPE DIEM:

Stop by your local bookstore and choose a blank book you like the look and feel of. Visit a coffee shop on your way home and write your first entry while enjoying a beverage.

54.

ACKNOWLEDGE ALL THE LOSSES THIS DEATH HAS WROUGHT.

- When a child dies, you lose not only the physical presence of the child, but also a part of your self. Your child came from you and was a part of you. Many grieving parents say that part of them died, too.

- Many grieving parents also lose a sense of security. They feel betrayed and unsafe. The world is no longer a trustworthy place.

- One of the most difficult losses for grieving parents is the loss of hopes and dreams for the future. When a child dies, that child's future dies with him. Your dreams of attending his graduation or wedding, cherishing his children or simply spending time with him as you grow old are irrevocably shattered.

- Allowing yourself to acknowledge the many levels of loss the death has brought to your life will help you move forward in your grief journey.

CARPE DIEM:
Name the things that you've lost or events you'll mourn in the future as a result of your child's death.

55.

ORGANIZE A TREE PLANTING.

- Trees represent the beauty, vibrancy and continuity of life.

- A specially planted and located tree can honor your child and serve as a perennial memorial. Maybe your child had a favorite tree—one he liked to climb or play near. Consider donating this variety of tree to a local park, school or library.

- You might write a short ceremony for the tree planting. (Or ask a friend or clergyperson to write and lead one.) Consider a personalized metal marker or sign, too.

- For a more private option, plant a tree in your own yard. Consult your local nursery for an appropriate selection. Flowering trees are especially beautiful in the spring. Trees with vibrant fall colors are another excellent choice. What type of tree reminds you most of your child?

CARPE DIEM:
Order a tree for your own yard and plant it in honor of your child. You'll probably need someone to help you prepare the hole and place the tree.

56.

PLAN A CEREMONY.

- A wise person once said: When words are inadequate, have ceremony.

- Ceremony assists in reality, recall, support, expression and transcendence.

- When personalized, the funeral ceremony can be a healing ritual. But ceremonies that take place later on can also be very meaningful.

- The ceremony might center on memories of your child, "meaning of life" thoughts and feelings or affirmation of faith.

CARPE DIEM:

Hold a candle-lighting memory ceremony. Invite a small group of friends and family who loved the child. Form a circle around a center candle, with each person holding their own small candle. Have each person light their candle from the center candle and share a memory of the child. At the end, play a song or read a poem or prayer.

57.

ORGANIZE A MEMORY BOOK.

- Assembling a scrapbook that holds treasured photos and mementos of your child can be a very healing activity.

- You might consider including her birth certificate, schoolwork, artwork, newspaper clippings, locks of hair, ticket stubs, award ribbons or certificates, etc.

- This activity can be just for you or for your whole family. You might be surprised how much your spouse and surviving children enjoy it once everyone gets started.

- Phone others who loved your child and ask them to write a note for the scrapbook or contribute photos.

- Once it's finished, you might display the memory book on a special easel or stand in your family room.

- Other ideas: a memory box, photo buttons of the child, a memory quilt.

CARPE DIEM:

Buy an appropriate scrapbook or keepsake box today. Don't forget to buy the associated materials you'll need, such as photo pages or photo corners, glue, scissors, etc.

58.

SUBSCRIBE TO HEALING.

- There are a number of healing magazines for mourners. Most include mourner's stories of loss and renewed hope, poetry, meaningful artwork.

- One of this author's favorites is *Bereavement*, a bimonthly magazine filled with personal stories of loss and healing, grief education, poetry, etc. The magazine is edited by Andrea Gambill, who wrote the Foreword for this book. At the time of this writing, a one-year subscription within the U.S. costs $32 and can be ordered through www.bereavementmag.com.

- Instead of a grief magazine, consider a magazine you've always wanted to read but have never allowed yourself the time to.

CARPE DIEM:
Start a subscription today.

59.

DON'T BE ALARMED
BY "GRIEFBURSTS."

- Sometimes heightened periods of sadness overwhelm grieving parents. These times can seem to come of out nowhere and can be frightening and painful.

- Even long after the death, something as simple as a sound, a smell or a phrase can bring on a "griefburst." You might hear a name, see a toy, or touch a fabric that suddenly reminds you of your child and all you have lost.

- Allow yourself to experience griefbursts without shame or self-judgment, no matter where and when they occur. (Sooner or later, one will probably happen when you're surrounded by people, maybe even strangers.) If you would feel more comfortable, retreat to somewhere private when these strong feelings surface.

- Don't isolate yourself in an attempt to protect yourself from griefbursts. Staying cooped up at home all the time is not self-compassion, it's self-destruction.

CARPE DIEM:
Create an action plan for your next griefburst. For example, you might plan to drop whatever you are doing and go for a walk or record thoughts in your journal.

60.

THINK YOUNG.

- It is the nature of children to live for the moment and appreciate today. All of us would benefit from a little more childlike wonder.

- Do something childish—blow bubbles, skip rope, visit a toy store, build a sand castle, fly a kite, climb a tree.

- If young children aren't a part of your life right now, make arrangements to spend some time with them. Volunteer at a local school. Take a friend's children to the park one afternoon.

- Think about what your child was like when he was very young. What made him laugh? What made him squeal with delight? What made him feel safe, content and loved?

CARPE DIEM:
Buy a gift for a child today just because.

61.

FOLLOW YOUR NOSE.

- For centuries people have understood that certain smells induce certain feelings. Aromatherapy is the contemporary term for this age-old practice.

- Some comforting, memory-inducing smells include baby powder, freshly cut grass, pine, chicken soup, popcorn.

- Essential oils, available at your local drugstore or bath and body shop, can be added to bath water or dabbed lightly on pulse points.

- Lavender relaxes. Rosewood and bergamot together lift the spirits. Peppermint invigorates. Chamomile and lavender are sleep aids.

CARPE DIEM:
Visit a local bath and body shop and choose one or two
essential oils or scented candles. Try using them today.

62.

LISTEN TO THE MUSIC.

- Music can be very healing to mourners because it helps us access our feelings, both happy and sad. Music can soothe the spirit and nurture the heart.

- All types of music can be healing—rock & roll, classical, blues, folk.

- Consider listening to music you normally don't, perhaps the opera or the symphony. Or make a recording of your favorite songs, all together on one tape or CD.

- Do you play an instrument or sing? Allow yourself the time to try these activities again soon.

- What kind of music did your child love? Have you listened to it lately? Get out her old cassettes or CDs and spend a rainy afternoon really listening to the music.

- Because music is the language of the soul, it can also be painful at times. If music brings comfort, then listen. If not, don't.

CARPE DIEM:
Visit a music store today and sample a few CDs or cassettes.
Buy yourself the one that moves you the most.

63.

PRAY.

- Prayer often comes naturally for grieving parents. At night when you go to bed and in the morning when you wake up, where else is there to turn for the kind of help you need? If you feel unable to pray, you might ask others to pray on your behalf.

- Besides, studies have shown that prayer can actually help people heal.

- If you believe in a higher power, pray. Pray for your child. Pray for your questions about life and death to be answered. Pray for the strength to embrace your pain and to heal over time. Pray for others affected by this death.

- Many places of worship have prayer lists. Call your place of worship and ask that your name be added to the prayer list. On worship day, the whole congregation will pray for you. Often many individuals will pray at home for those on the prayer list, as well.

- Some faiths have ongoing prayers that are said for the dead. Mourning Jews (traditionally males) say a special daily prayer called the Kaddish. Perhaps creating a daily prayer ritual—designating a time, place and prayer to say each day—would provide a systematic and healing outlet for your grief.

CARPE DIEM:

Bow your head right now and say a silent prayer. If you are out of practice, don't worry; just let your thoughts flow naturally.

64.

LEARN SOMETHING NEW.

- Sometimes grieving parents feel stuck. They can feel depressed and the daily routine of their lives can be joyless.

- Perhaps you would enjoy learning something new or trying a new hobby.

- What have you always wanted to learn but have never tried? Playing the guitar? Woodworking? Speaking French? Many grieving parents have taught me that they no longer fear failure because what is failure compared to what they've experienced? So if you're no longer afraid to fail, you might be ready to give a new activity a try.

- Consider physical activities. Learning to play golf or taking part in karate have the added benefits of exercise.

- Learning something new together is a way for some grieving spouses to reconnect and to rebuild their lives. Take a class or lessons in something neither of you has ever done before.

CARPE DIEM:
Get ahold of your local community calendar and sign up for a class in something you have never tried before.

65.

TAKE A RISK.

- For some, activities that harbor risk, real or perceived, are invigorating and life-affirming.

- Sometimes people who've encountered death, in particular, feel ready to try limit-stretching activities.

- Some ideas: hang gliding, bungee jumping, skydiving, rock climbing.

- Other, less physical risky activities might include traveling to a foreign country, singing or speaking in front of a crowd, and learning to pilot a plane.

- Don't confuse appropriate risk-taking with self-destructiveness. Never test your own mortality through inappropriate behaviors or inadequate safeguards.

CARPE DIEM:
Schedule a sunrise hot air balloon ride with a trained, licensed balloonist. Toast the dawn with champagne at 3,000 feet.

66.

PICTURE THIS.

- The visual arts have a way of making us see the world anew.

- Perhaps you would enjoy a visit to an art gallery or museum, a sculpture garden, a photography exhibit. Did your child like artwork? What kind did he like to look at or create? Frame your favorite piece of your child's artwork.

- Why not try to create some art yourself? Attend a watercolor or calligraphy class. Creating artwork is a great way to express your grief.

- Making pottery is something almost everyone enjoys. It's tactile and messy and whimsical.

CARPE DIEM:
Buy some paints, some brushes and a canvas and paint your feelings about the death. Don't worry about your artistic abilities; just let your imagination take charge.

67.

HELP OTHERS.

- Help others! But I'm the one who needs help right now, you may be thinking.

- It's true, you do deserve special compassion and attention right now. But often, people find healing in selflessness.

- What made you most proud to be your child's parent? Maybe you can translate your child's legacy into a way to help others.

- If you're well into your grief journey, you may find yourself ready and able to help other mourners by starting a support group or volunteering at a hospice. Many grieving parents are active in The Compassionate Friends, leading their local chapters and playing an active role in helping newly bereaved families.

CARPE DIEM:
Do something nice for someone else today,
maybe someone who doesn't really deserve it.

68.

VOLUNTEER.

- Consider honoring your child's death through social activism. If she was a victim of drunk driving, participate in a local MADD rally. If she died of cancer, volunteer for your local hospice.

- Many grieving parents find that they get much more out of their volunteer efforts than they put in. And volunteering is also a way of affirming the preciousness of life.

- Consider volunteering together with your partner and/or surviving children. Volunteering as a family is a good way to strengthen the ties that bind.

- If your schedule is too hectic, offer money instead of time. Make your donation in memory of your child.

CARPE DIEM:
Call your local United Way and ask for some suggestions about upcoming events you could participate in.

69.

LAUGH.

- Humor is one of the most healing gifts of humanity.

- Laughter restores hope and assists us in surviving the pain of grief. If you're of faith, perhaps you'll relate to Proverbs 15:13: A merry heart is good medicine for the soul.

- It's OK to laugh even though your child is dead. You can laugh and still love and miss your child very much. In fact, laughing is a way of honoring the child's spirit.

- What made your child laugh? Silly jokes? Slapstick comedy? Intellectual humor?

CARPE DIEM:

Try to remember one time in particular that your child laughed and laughed. Close your eyes and immerse yourself in this moment. See if you can recall your child's face and the sound of his laughter.

70.

VISIT THE GREAT OUTDOORS.

- For many people it is restorative and energizing to spend time outside.

- Mourners often find nature's timeless beauty healing. The sound of a bird singing or the awesome presence of rock outcroppings can help put things in perspective.

- Go on a nature walk. Or camping. Or canoeing. The farther away from civilization the better.

- Where did your child like to be outdoors? Have you visited this place recently? If not, make a point to spend some time there in the near future.

- Experience the elements. Take time to feel the rain, wind or snow.

CARPE DIEM:
Call your area forest service for a map of nearby walking or hiking trails. Take a hike sometime this week.

71.

BRIGHTEN UP YOUR ENVIRONMENT.

- Would your home or office benefit from a little sprucing up?

- When you're feeling you have some energy, paint your living room or office in a fresh, new color. Paint is inexpensive and easy to redo. Ask a friend to help you take this on. Have fun with it!

- Sometimes something as minor as new pillows or freshly cleaned windowpanes can make a big difference.

- Be bold and decisive. Taking charge of your environment is one way to feel like you're taking charge of your life.

CARPE DIEM:
The principles of feng shui encourage you to paint your front door a shade of red. This color is supposed to be welcoming and bring positive energy into your house. What the heck; give it a try.

72.

SIMPLIFY YOUR LIFE.

- Many of us today are taking stock of what's really important in our lives and trying to discard the rest.

- Grieving parents are often overwhelmed by all the tasks and commitments they have. If you can rid yourself of some of those extraneous burdens, you'll have more time for your family and for mourning and healing.

- What is it that is overburdening you right now? Have your name taken off junk mail lists, ignore your dirty house, stop attending any optional meetings you don't look forward to.

- Ask a friend to help you with running errands, getting groceries, paying bills, etc. Lots of times your friends would like to help but don't know how. This is one practical, tangible way they can.

CARPE DIEM:

Have a family meeting and take stock of your activities calendar. Ask everyone which activities they truly want to continue and which they would be happier without. Make cuts where appropriate. Maybe you can even fill in some of the extra time you'll have with a little vacation.

73.

ESTABLISH A MEMORIAL FUND IN THE NAME OF YOUR CHILD.

- Sometimes bereaved families ask that memorial contributions be made to specified charities in the name of the child who died. This practice allows friends and family members to show their support while helping the family feel that something good came of the death.

- You can establish a personalized and ongoing memorial to the child who died, even if you're not wealthy. Some parents organize yearly yard sales. Some establish scholarship funds. Some donate each year to a certain charity. Some establish school awards in their child's name. Consider being the one to present the award or scholarship to the recipients.

- What was meaningful to your child? Did she love a sport or a hobby? Did she have empathy for a certain group of people? Was she affected by a certain illness?

- Your local bank or funeral home may have ideas about how to go about setting up a memorial fund.

CARPE DIEM:
Call a friend or talk to your family and together brainstorm a list of ideas for a memorial. Then take it one step further and make a phone call for additional information.

74.

TALK TO A COUNSELOR.

- While grief counseling is not for everyone, many grieving parents are helped through their grief journeys by a compassionate counselor.

- If possible, find a counselor who has experience with grief and loss issues. Not all counselors are good at helping those who mourn. In fact, some are downright lousy at it. If you start seeing a counselor who doesn't seem to be helpful after several sessions, it's OK to find a different one.

- As with a support group, you may be more ready for counseling six months to a year after the death than you are immediately after. And it's never too late to see a counselor, even years or decades after your child's death.

- Ask your friends for referrals to a counselor they've been helped by.

- A clergyperson may also be a good person to talk to during this time, but only if he affirms your need to mourn this death and search for meaning. Believing in God and an afterlife does not mean you shouldn't mourn!

CARPE DIEM:
Schedule an initial interview with at least two counselors so you can see whom you're most comfortable with.

75.

WATCH FOR WARNING SIGNS.

- Understandably, sometimes grieving parents fall back on self-destructive behaviors to get through this difficult time.

- Try to be honest with yourself about drug or alcohol abuse. If you're in over your head, ask someone for help. If others approach you about your substance abuse, let them in.

- Of course, mental illness and personality problems that were present before the death can also complicate grief.

- Seeing a grief counselor is probably a good idea for parents who are also struggling with substance abuse, clinical depression or other mental health-related problem. They may simply not be able to reconcile their grief and continue their lives in meaningful ways without professional help.

- Are you seriously considering suicide? Put this book down right now and talk to someone about your depression.

CARPE DIEM:
Acknowledging to ourselves that we have a problem may come too late. If someone suggests that you need help, consider yourself lucky to be so well-loved and get help.

76.

LOOK INTO SUPPORT GROUPS.

- Grief support groups are a healing, safe place for many mourners to express their thoughts and feelings. Grieving parents, in particular, often find genuine understanding and comfort in support groups comprised of grieving parents that they can't find anywhere else.

- Sharing similar experiences with other grieving parents may help you feel like you're not alone, that you're not going crazy.

- Your local hospice or funeral home may offer a free or low-cost support group. The Compassionate Friends may also have a local chapter.

- If you are newly bereaved, you may not feel ready for a support group. Many mourners are more open to joining a support group six-nine months after the death. You will know when and if you feel ready to join a support group.

- When to stop going to a support group is another question many grieving parents have. Sometimes, you just know it's time for you to graduate. Other times you may want to stay around to support more newly bereaved parents. The only good answer to this question is whenever the group begins to feel less helpful, less relevant or more of a burden than a help. Sometimes certain group members affect the group's dynamic in harmful ways. In this case, starting a different group is also an option.

CARPE DIEM:
Call around today for support group information. If you're feeling ready, plan to attend a meeting this week or next.

77.

PREPARE YOURSELF FOR THE HOLIDAYS.

- Because your child is no longer there to share the holidays with, you may feel particularly sad and vulnerable during Thanksgiving, Christmas, Hanukkah, Easter and other holidays.

- Don't overextend yourself during the holidays. Don't feel you have to shop, bake, entertain, send cards, etc. if you're not up for it.

- Sometimes old holiday rituals are comforting after a death and sometimes they're not. Continue them only if they feel good to you; consider creating new ones, as well.

- Finding a way to make your child part of your holiday ritual might help you feel like the holidays are more whole. For example, you could decorate a small, table-top tree each year in honor of the child who died. On the tree, hang ornaments the child made, photos of the child, special mementos, rattles or other little toys, etc. Ask someone to help you with this project.

CARPE DIEM:
What's the next major holiday? Make a game plan right now and let those you usually spend the day with know of your plan well in advance.

78.

FIND A GRIEF "BUDDY."

- Though no one else will grieve this death just as you do, other grieving parents have had similar experiences.

- Find a grief "buddy"—someone who is also in mourning, someone you can talk to, someone who also needs a companion in grief right now.

- Make a pact with your grief buddy to call each other whenever one of you needs to talk. Promise to listen without judgment. Commit to spending time together.

- You might arrange to meet once a week for breakfast or lunch with your grief buddy.

CARPE DIEM:
Do you know another grieving parent who also needs grief support right now? Call her and ask her out to lunch today. If it feels right, discuss the possibility of being grief buddies.

79.

DO SOMETHING YOU'RE GOOD AT.

- Often it helps mourners to affirm their worth to others and to themselves.

- Do something you're good at, even if at first you don't feel like it. Ride a bike. Go for a swim. Bake a cake. Do the crossword puzzle. Write a poem. Tell a joke. Play with your surviving children. Balance your checkbook. Talk to a friend. It feels good to accomplish, even if it's something small.

- Have other people told you you're good at this or that? Next time you're complimented in this way, take it to heart!

CARPE DIEM:

Make a list of ten things you're good at. Do one of them today and afterwards, reflect on how you feel.

80.

REACH OUT TO OTHERS FOR HELP.

- Perhaps the most compassionate thing you can do for yourself at this difficult time is to reach out for help from others.

- Think of it this way: Grieving may be the hardest work you have ever done. And hard work is less burdensome when others lend a hand. Life's greatest challenges—getting through school, raising children, pursuing a career—are in many ways team efforts. So it should be with mourning.

- Sharing your pain with others won't make it disappear, but it will, over time, make it more bearable.

- Reaching out for help also connects you to other people and strengthens the bonds of love that make life seem worth living again.

- When others ask you how you're doing, don't say, "I'm fine." Brutal honesty may open a helpful dialogue.

CARPE DIEM:

Call a close friend who may have distanced himself from you since the death and tell him how much you need him right now. Tell him specific ways he can help.

81.

SPEND TIME ALONE.

- Reaching out to others while we're in mourning is necessary. Mourning is hard work and you can't get through it by yourself.

- Still, you will also need alone time as you work on the six needs of mourning. To slow down and to turn inward, you must sometimes insist on solitude.

- Schedule alone time into each week. Go for a walk in the woods. Lock your bedroom door and read a book. Work in your garden.

- Don't shut your friends and family out altogether, but do heed the call for contemplative silence.

CARPE DIEM:
Schedule one hour of solitude into your day today.

82.

TALK OUT LOUD TO
THE CHILD WHO DIED.

- Sometimes it still feels good to talk to your child. Pretend she's sitting in the chair across from you and tell her how you're doing. Tell her you miss her.

- It may help to talk to photos of your child. Share your deepest thoughts and feelings with him. Make it part of your daily routine to say "Good morning!" to that photo on your nightstand.

- Visit the cemetery and if you're not too self-conscious, talk to your child.

- Or talk silently to your child when you go to bed each night.

CARPE DIEM:
If you haven't already, put a photo of your child who died in your wallet or purse. Make it a habit to look at the photo and tell her what's going on in your life that day.

83.

KNOW THAT IT'S NORMAL TO FEEL THE PRESENCE OF YOUR CHILD.

- Sometimes, grieving parents tell me that they have felt the presence of their child. They have been going about some everyday activity and suddenly felt their child was in the room. Or they have had a vivid dream in which their child tells them what heaven is like. Or something unusual happens and the parents perceive it as a sign from their child.

- These kinds of phenomena seem very real and are often very reassuring to grieving parents. If you've felt your child's presence, you're not crazy. Who's to say what's real and what's imagined? What matters is your love for your child and your continued feelings of connection to him.

- If you've felt the presence of your child since his death, tell someone (preferably someone who's open-minded) about it. Often such experiences are welcomed by others because they reassure us all that death may not be the end.

CARPE DIEM:

If you've felt the presence of your child since his death, write down your story and share it with someone close to you. Or tuck the story away with your private papers so that your loved ones can one day be comforted by it.

84.

SET ASIDE THE ANNIVERSARY OF THE DEATH AS A HOLIDAY.

- Perhaps you dread the anniversary of your child's death. Many mourners feel particularly sad and helpless on this day.

- Consider setting aside the anniversary as an annual holiday. Each year, visit the grave. Perhaps plan a ceremony with friends and family.

- Commemorate the life that was lived by doing something the child would appreciate.

- You might want to spend this day in the company of others who love you.

- Some grieving parents have a harder time with the days leading up to the anniversary of the death or the days immediately following. If this is true for you, make plans to be with people who care about you during this time.

CARPE DIEM:
Call three other people who loved the child
and plan an activity for the anniversary of the death.

85.

CELEBRATE THE BIRTHDAY OF THE CHILD WHO DIED.

- Your child's birthday—what a special day in your life. You remember the amazing day your child was born, you remember each birthday she was with you, and now you are confronted with each birthday she will never have.

- Some parents find comfort in continuing to celebrate the birthday of their child, perhaps with a visit to the cemetery or a trip to a certain park or restaurant. The celebration helps them feel that they are keeping their child's memory alive.

- As time passes, it's not unusual for grieving parents to "stop the clock." Parents often think of young children who died as continuing to get older: "Molly would have been eight today." But at some point, time seems to stand still, and from that moment forward, parents often think of their child as a teenager or young adult forevermore. This is a common phenomenon and perfectly normal.

CARPE DIEM:

Consider honoring your child's birthday by giving a gift each year in her memory. Donate a toy to a family shelter or a special book to the library. Shop for a special present and give it anonymously to someone who would appreciate it. Begin planning your new birthday tradition today.

86.

TAKE A MINI-VACATION.

- Don't have time to take time off? Plan several mini-vacations this month instead.

- What creative ideas can you come up with to renew yourself? Here are a few ideas to get you started.
  - Schedule a massage with a professional massage therapist.
  - Have a spiritual growth weekend. Retreat into nature. Plan some alone time. Go somewhere quiet to think about your child.
  - Go for a drive with no particular destination in mind. Explore the countryside, slow down and observe what you see.
  - Treat yourself to a night in a hotel or bed and breakfast.
  - Visit a museum or a zoo.
  - Go to a yard sale or auction.
  - Go roller-skating or roller-blading with a friend.
  - Drop by a health food store and walk the aisles.

- Remember—you can have fun and grieve for your child at the same time. Don't feel guilty for needing a break; it will help you survive and revive.

CARPE DIEM:
Plan a mini-vacation for today. Spend
one hour doing something special.

87.

RECONNECT WITH SOMEONE SPECIAL.

- Throughout our lives, we often lose contact with people who've touched us or made a difference somehow.

- Death can make us realize that keeping in touch with these people is well worth the effort.

- Whom have you loved or admired but haven't spoken with for a long time?

- To wit: teachers, old lovers, childhood friends, past neighbors,

- Think about a person who made a difference in the life of your child. Have you talked to this person lately?

CARPE DIEM:
Write a letter to someone you haven't been in touch
with for a long time. Track down his address and phone
number. Catch him up on your life and invite him
to do the same by calling you or writing you back.

88.

RELEASE ANY BAD FEELINGS OR REGRETS YOU MAY HAVE ABOUT THE FUNERAL AND BURIAL.

- The funeral is a wonderful means of expressing our beliefs, thoughts and feelings about the death of someone loved.

- Funerals help us acknowledge the reality of the death, give testimony to the life of the person who died, express our grief, support each other and embrace our faith and beliefs about life and death

- Yet for many grieving parents, the death of a child came without warning. Funeral and burial decisions had to be made quickly, while the parents were still in deep shock and disbelief. Sometimes some of these decisions seem wrong with the benefit of hindsight.

- If you harbor any negative feelings about your child's funeral or memorial service, know this: You and everyone else who was a part of the service did the best they could do at the time. You cannot change what happened, but you can talk about what happened and share your thoughts and feelings with someone who cares. Don't berate yourself.

- It's never too late to hold another memorial service for your child. Perhaps a tree-planting ceremony or a small gathering on the anniversary of the child's death could be a forum for sharing memories and prayer. Ask a clergyperson or someone you know to be a good public speaker to help plan and lead the ceremony.

CARPE DIEM:
If you harbor regrets or anger about your child's funeral and burial, talk about these feelings with someone today. Perhaps the two of you together can create an "action plan" to help make things better.

89.

REMEMBER OTHERS WHO HAD A SPECIAL RELATIONSHIP WITH YOUR CHILD.

- At times your appropriately inward focus will make you feel alone in your grief. Grieving parents, especially, are often so immersed in their own grief in the early weeks and months after the death that they cannot empathize with others who loved the child.

- Maybe you're ready to think about others who were affected by the death of your child: friends, boyfriends or girlfriends, teachers, neighbors, coworkers.

- Is there someone outside of the inner "circle of mourners" who may be struggling with this death? Perhaps you could write her a note of support and thanks for the love and friendship she gave to your child.

- Grieving children especially need our love and support. If your child was young when she died, her friends need opportunities to mourn. Maybe you could invite her friends to your house or take them shopping for an afternoon. With their parents' permission, talk to them about the death and their thoughts and feelings.

CARPE DIEM:
Today, write and mail a brief supportive note
to someone else affected by the death.

90.

ALLOW FOR FEELINGS OF UNFINISHED BUSINESS.

- Death often brings about feelings of unfinished business. Things we never did, things we didn't get to say, things we wish we hadn't.

- Allow yourself to think and feel through these "if onlys." You may never be able to fully resolve these issues, but if you permit yourself to mourn them, you will become reconciled to them.

- Is there something you wanted to say to the child who died but never did? Is there something that happened that you regret? Write him a letter that openly expresses your thoughts and feelings.

CARPE DIEM:
Perhaps the child who died left some task or goal
incomplete. Finish it on his behalf.

91.

SCHEDULE SOMETHING THAT GIVES YOU PLEASURE EACH AND EVERY DAY.

- Often grieving parents struggle with getting up in the morning. When they awaken, even if they've had a peaceful night's sleep, they're confronted with the brutal reality that their child is gone forever.

- It's hard to look forward to each day when you know you will be experiencing pain and sadness. To counterbalance your normal and necessary mourning, give yourself a reason to get out of the bed in the morning.

- Reading, baking, going for a walk, having lunch with a friend, playing computer games—whatever brings you enjoyment.

- On the flip side, many grieving parents also feel guilty about having fun or experiencing any pleasure. I must be an awful person if I can have fun when my child is dead, they think. If I have fun, that must mean I didn't totally love my child. Or: My child is dead and has been deprived of the pleasures of life. What right do I have to experience pleasure?

- Over time you'll come to realize that seeking happiness does not diminish your love for your child; the two can and should coexist. Like many grieving parents, you may also grow to believe that you owe it your child to make the most of each and every day.

CARPE DIEM:
What's on tap for today? Plan on doing something you enjoy, no matter how hectic your schedule.

92.

JOIN THE CLUB.

- You may benefit from regular participation in social organizations because they provide friendship, routine and plans for the future.

- Book discussion groups, Kiwanis, singing groups, and environmental organizations are just a few ideas.

- Political groups and human service organizations (Sierra Club, United Way, etc.) can provide a sense of purpose and satisfaction.

- A number of organizations offer regular meetings and activities for grieving parents. These include The Compassionate Friends, Parents of Murdered Children and MADD. At some point in their grief journeys, most grieving parents find the sharing and camaraderie provided by these groups to be profoundly helpful.

CARPE DIEM:
Check your local paper for a listing of club and organization meetings. Circle two or three and call the contact person for more information.

93.

TEACH OTHERS ABOUT GRIEF AND MOURNING.

- To love is to one day mourn. You have learned this most poignant of life's lessons.

- Maybe you could teach what you are learning to others. Tell your friends and family about the six needs of mourning. Teach them how they can best support you.

- Share your wisdom in the safety of a grief support group.

- Remember that each person's grief is unique. Your experiences will not be shared or appreciated by everyone.

CARPE DIEM:
Buy a friend the companion book to this one, called *Healing A Friend's Grieving Heart: 100 Practical Ideas For Helping Someone You Love Through Loss*. It provides concise grief education and practical tips for helping.

94.

EXPRESS YOUR FAITH.

- Above all, mourning is a spiritual journey of the heart and soul. The death of a child gives rise to the most profound spiritual yearnings and chaos. It is important to begin to examine your beliefs about death and develop an understanding of where God is in your suffering.

- If you have faith or spirituality, express it in ways that seem appropriate to you.

- Attending church or your place of worship, reading religious texts and praying are a few conventional ways of expressing your faith. Be open to less conventional ways, as well, such as meditating or spending time alone in nature.

- For many grieving parents, having faith means feeling sure that they will one day see their child again. This belief alone, whether in heaven, reincarnation or a less defined kind of afterlife, makes life bearable. Do you believe you will be reunited with your child one day? If you do, allow yourself to revel in its comforts. Close your eyes and envision your concept of heaven. See your child smiling at you, welcoming you, reaching out to hold you. Retreat to this image when you are sad or disheartened.

CARPE DIEM:
Visit your place of worship today, either for services
or for an informal time of prayer and solitude.

95.

IDENTIFY THREE PEOPLE YOU CAN TURN TO ANYTIME YOU NEED A FRIEND.

- You may have many people who care about you but few who are able to be good companions in grief.

- Identify three people whom you think can be there for you in the coming weeks, months and years.

- Don't assume that others will help. Even normally compassionate people sometimes find it hard to be present to others in grief.

- If some of your closest friends seem to have abandoned you, don't give up on them. They probably just need you to take the lead in teaching them how to be a friend in grief. Invite one or two of them to lunch; be candid about your feelings and how they can help.

CARPE DIEM:

Call these three people and ask them outright: Will you help me? Tell them you mainly need to spend time with them and be able to talk to them freely.

96.

GET A NEW HAIRCUT, HIGHLIGHT OR COLOR.

- Sometimes when we're in mourning we feel dull and unattractive. Our self-esteem can be affected by our grief.

- You may not be bothering with your appearance right now because of your low energy. And besides, you might be telling yourself, what does it matter what I look like? It's not always bad to look bad, because it allows others to see how you feel on the inside.

- Yet part of good self-care and healing is learning to love and value our lives again, including our physical selves. This doesn't mean you should be vain and shallow. It just means that your soul isn't the only facet of your being that needs attention.

- Take a look in the mirror and compassionately reacquaint yourself with you.

CARPE DIEM:
Today, schedule an appointment for a new haircut, highlight or color. Get a facial and manicure, too, if your budget permits.

97.

REASSESS YOUR PRIORITIES.

- Death has a way of making us rethink our lives and the meaningfulness of the ways we spend them. The death of a child, in particular, tends to awaken grieving parents to what is truly meaningful in life.

- What gives your life meaning? What doesn't? Take steps to spend more of your time on the former and less on the latter.

- Now may be the time to reconfigure your life. Choose a satisfying new career. Go back to school. Begin volunteering. Help others in regular, ongoing ways. Move closer to your surviving children.

- Many grieving parents have told me that they can no longer stand to be around people who seem shallow, egocentric, or mean-spirited. It's OK to let friendships wither with friends whom these adjectives now seem to describe. Instead, find ways to connect with people who share your new outlook on life—and death.

CARPE DIEM:

Make a list with two columns: What's important to me. What's not. Brainstorm for at least 15 minutes.

98.

MAKE A LIST OF GOALS.

- While you should not set a particular time and course for your healing, it may help you to have made other life goals for the coming year.

- Make a list of short-term goals for the next three months. Perhaps some of the goals could have to do with mourning activities (e.g., make a memory book).

- Also make a list of long-term goals for the next year. Be both realistic and compassionate with yourself as you consider what's feasible and feels good and what will only add too much stress to your life.

- What were your child's goals or dreams in life? Can you find a way to begin to integrate some of those goals or dreams into your life?

CARPE DIEM:

Write a list of goals for this week. Your goals may be as simple as: Go to work every day. Tell John I love him once a day. Take a walk on Tuesday night.

99.

UNDERSTAND THE CONCEPT OF "RECONCILIATION."

- Sometimes you'll hear about mourners "recovering" from or "getting over" grief. These terms are damaging because they imply that grief is an illness that must be cured. It also connotes an eventual return to the way things were before the death.

- Having been a parent is a permanent change in a man or woman's life. Just as parents don't get over being a parent, they don't get over their grief. Instead, they become "reconciled" to it. In other words, they learn to live with it and are forever changed by it.

- This does not mean a life of misery, however. Mourners often not only heal but grow through grief. Our lives can potentially be deeper and more meaningful after the death of someone loved.

- In reconciliation, the sharp pangs of grief soften and painful thoughts and feelings subside. A renewed interest in the future begins to overtake that natural obsession with the past. Days are happier than sad. New goals are set and worked toward. Bonds with other people are strengthened and enjoyed. Hope is renewed.

CARPE DIEM:
Have you begun to reconcile your grief? If so, what does reconciliation feel like for you?

100.

EMBRACE THE WAYS IN WHICH YOU ARE GROWING THROUGH GRIEF.

- You may find that you are growing emotionally and spiritually as a result of your grief journey. I understand that you've paid the ultimate price for this growth and that you would gladly trade it for one more minute with your child. Still, the death may have brought bittersweet gifts into your life that you would not otherwise have.

- Many grieving parents emerge from the early years of grief as stronger, more capable people. They're more assertive and apt to say what they really believe and be who they are. They don't put up with baloney. They've already survived the worst life has to offer, so anything still to come can't be so bad. And they've learned what's truly important and what's not.

- What's more, many grieving parents discover depths of compassion for others that they never knew they had. Lots volunteer, many undertake daily kindnesses, virtually all are more emotionally and spiritually tuned-in to others and more interpersonally effective.

CARPE DIEM:
Consider the ways in which you may be
"growing through grief."

A FINAL WORD

But grief still has to be worked through. It is like walking through water.
Sometimes there is an enormous breaker that knocks me down. Sometimes
there is a sudden and fierce squall. But I know that many waters cannot
quench love, neither can the floods drown it.

Madeleine L'Engle

As you know, you are a different person than you were before your child died. You have been knocked down, but not knocked out. You have been damaged, but not defeated.

In the beginning of this book I wrote, "You have a broken heart. I truly believe that acknowledging your heart is broken is the beginning of your healing. As you experience the pain of your loss—gently opening, acknowledging and allowing—, the suffering it has wrought diminishes, but never completely vanishes." Yes, in loving your precious child, you opened yourself to life's greatest hurt, but also to life's greatest love. As your experience of reconciliation unfolds, you will recognize that life is and will continue to be different without the presence of your child.

Yet grieving parents have taught me about courage and perseverance. The parents of the four children to whose memory this book is dedicated are living testimony to this reality. While these parents were naturally "broken" in the early days of their grief journeys, today they are new people with so much to give to their "fellow strugglers." They have suffered deeply through the early years of their grief and now, though they still grieve and always will, they have become caregivers, world-changers and true lovers of life.

Andrea and Jim Gambill developed the wonderful and healing *Bereavement* magazine. Ros and Glenn Crichton founded The Coping Centre, a sacred retreat center for grieving parents. Nancy and Gary Zastrow created *Wings*, a quarterly newsletter for grieving people. And Bonnie and Tony Redfern completed their Death and Grief Studies

Certificates as well as masters degrees and have supported many other people in grief. So, as you can see, these couples have honored their heart-rending grief and gone on to transform not only their own lives but the lives of literally thousands of other bereaved parents!

Grieving parents like the Gambills, the Crichtons, the Zastrows and the Redferns have taught me so much.

Grieving parents have taught me to slow down, to enjoy the moment, to find hidden treasures everywhere—a beautiful sunrise, a flower in bloom, a hike in the woods, a friend's gentle touch, a child's smile.

Grieving parents have taught me that there is so much to learn about ourselves and the world around us. They have taught me to live fully in the present while remembering my past and embracing my future.

Grieving parents have taught me to be open to giving and receiving love. They have taught me to seek a sense of belonging, a sense of meaning, a sense of purpose both in my life's work and in my relationships with family and friends. They have taught me there are magic and miracles in loving and being loved.

Most important, grieving parents have taught me so very much about what it means to love a child. Your lessons have permeated my soul and my ways of being with my own three children. I thank God for every day I have on this earth with them.

I often say that to mourn well is to live and love well again. Will you truly live or will you merely exist? Choosing to mourn openly, honestly and authentically is, ultimately, to choose life and to discover hope, which is an expectation of a good that is yet to be. My desire is that this book has brought you some element of hope.

Just one more thing: Right now, take a moment to close your eyes, open your heart, and remember your child's precious smile.

Bless you. I hope we meet one day.

THE MOURNER'S CODE
Ten Self-Compassionate Principles

Though you should reach out to others as you journey through grief, you should not feel obligated to accept the unhelpful responses you may receive from some people. You are the one who is grieving, and as such, you have certain "rights" no one should try to take away from you.

The following list is intended both to empower you to heal and to decide how others can and cannot help. This is not to discourage you from reaching out to others for help, but rather to assist you in distinguishing useful responses from hurtful ones.

1. You have the right to experience your own unique grief.

No one else will grieve in exactly the same way you do. So, when you turn to others for help, don't allow them to tell you what you should or should not be feeling.

2. You have the right to talk about your grief.

Talking about your grief will help you heal. Seek out others who will allow you to talk as much as you want, as often as you want, about your grief. If at times you don't feel like talking, you also have the right to be silent.

3. You have the right to feel a multitude of emotions.

Confusion, disorientation, fear, guilt and relief are just a few of the emotions you might feel as part of your grief journey. Others may try to tell you that feeling angry, for example, is wrong. Don't take these judgmental responses to heart. Instead, find listeners who will accept your feelings without condition.

4. You have the right to be tolerant of your physical and emotional limits.

Your feelings of loss and sadness will probably leave you feeling fatigued. Respect what your body and mind are telling you. Get daily rest. Eat balanced meals. And don't allow others to push you into doing things you don't feel ready to do.

5. You have the right to experience "griefbursts."
Sometimes, out of nowhere, a powerful surge of grief may overcome you. This can be frightening, but it is normal and natural. Find someone who understands and will let you talk it out.

6. You have the right to make use of ritual.
The funeral ritual does more than acknowledge the death of someone loved. It helps provide you with the support of caring people. More importantly, the funeral is a way for you to mourn. If others tell you the funeral or other healing rituals such as these are silly or unnecessary, don't listen.

7. You have the right to embrace your spirituality.
If faith is a part of your life, express it in ways that seem appropriate to you. Allow yourself to be around people who understand and support your religious beliefs. If you feel angry at God, find someone to talk with who won't be critical of your feelings of hurt and abandonment.

8. You have the right to search for meaning.
You may find yourself asking, "Why did he or she die? Why this way? Why now?" Some of your questions may have answers, but some may not. And watch out for the clichéd responses some people may give you. Comments like, "It was God's will" or "Think of what you still have to be thankful for" are not helpful and you do not have to accept them.

9. You have the right to treasure your memories.
Memories are one of the best legacies that exist after the death of someone loved. You will always remember. Instead of ignoring your memories, find others with whom you can share them.

10. You have the right to move toward your grief and heal.
Reconciling your grief will not happen quickly. Remember, grief is a process, not an event. Be patient and tolerant with yourself and avoid people who are impatient and intolerant with you. Neither you nor those around you must forget that the death of someone loved changes your life forever.

SEND US YOUR IDEAS FOR HEALING A PARENT'S GRIEVING HEART!

I'd love to hear your practical ideas for being self-compassionate in grief. I may use them in future editions of this book or in other publications through the Center for Loss. Please jot down your idea and mail it to:

Dr. Alan Wolfelt
The Center for Loss and Life Transition
3735 Broken Bow Rd.
Fort Collins, CO 80526
wolfelt@centerforloss.com

I look forward to hearing from you!

My idea:

_____

_____

_____

_____

_____

_____

_____

My name and mailing address:

_____

_____

_____

ALSO BY ALAN WOLFELT

HEALING A FRIEND'S GRIEVING HEART: 100 PRACTICAL IDEAS FOR HELPING SOMEONE YOU LOVE THROUGH LOSS

When a friend suffers the loss of someone loved, you may not always know what to say: But you can *do* many helpful, loving things. Compassionate and eminently practical, *Healing A Friend's Grieving Heart* offers 100 fresh ideas for supporting a grieving friend or family member. Some of the ideas teach the fundamentals of grief and mourning, while others offer practical day-to-day ways to help. Turn to any page and seize the day by being a real friend in grief today, right now, right this minute.

ISBN 978-1-879651-26-5
128 pages • Softcover • $11.95
(plus additional shipping and handling)

Companion
PRESS

All Dr. Wolfelt's publications can be ordered by mail from:
Companion Press
3735 Broken Bow Road • Fort Collins, CO 80526
(970) 226-6050 • Fax 1-800-922-6051
www.centerforloss.com

ALSO BY ALAN WOLFELT

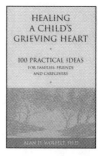

HEALING A CHILD'S GRIEVING HEART: 100 PRACTICAL IDEAS FOR FAMILIES, FRIENDS & CAREGIVERS

An idea book for grown-ups who want practical, day-to-day "how tos" for helping the grieving children they love. Some ideas teach about children's unique mourning styles and needs. Others suggest simple activities and tips for spending time together.

ISBN 978-1-879651-28-9 • 128 pages • Softcover • $11.95
(plus additional shipping and handling)

HEALING YOUR GRIEVING HEART FOR KIDS: 100 PRACTICAL IDEAS

Simple advice and activities for children after a death. An idea book for young and middle readers (6-12 year-olds) grieving the death of someone loved. The text is simple and straightforward,   teaching children about grief and affirming that their thoughts and feelings are not only normal but necessary. Page after page of age-appropriate activities and gentle, healing guidance.

ISBN 978-1-879651-27-2 • 128 pages • Softcover • $11.95
(plus additional shipping and handling)

Companion
PRESS

All Dr. Wolfelt's publications can be ordered by mail from:
Companion Press
3735 Broken Bow Road • Fort Collins, CO 80526
(970) 226-6050 • Fax 1-800-922-6051
www.centerforloss.com

ALSO BY ALAN WOLFELT

HEALING A TEEN'S GRIEVING HEART: 100 PRACTICAL IDEAS FOR FAMILIES, FRIENDS & CAREGIVERS

If you want to help a grieving teen but aren't sure how, this book is for you. It explains the teen's unique mourning needs, offers real-world advice and suggests realistic activities.

ISBN 978-1-879651-24-1
128 pages • Softcover • $11.95
(plus additional shipping and handling)

HEALING YOUR GRIEVING HEART FOR TEENS: 100 PRACTICAL IDEAS

Grief is especially difficult during the teen years. This book explains why this is so and offers straightforward, practical advice for healing

ISBN 978-1-879651-24-1
128 pages • Softcover • $11.95
(plus additional shipping and handling)

Companion
PRESS

All Dr. Wolfelt's publications can be ordered by mail from:
Companion Press
3735 Broken Bow Road • Fort Collins, CO 80526
(970) 226-6050 • Fax 1-800-922-6051
www.centerforloss.com

ALSO BY ALAN WOLFELT

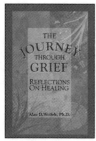

THE JOURNEY THROUGH GRIEF: REFLECTIONS ON HEALING
SECOND EDITION

This revised, second edition of *The Journey Through Grief* takes Dr. Wolfelt's popular book of reflections and adds space for guided journaling, asking readers thoughtful questions about their unique mourning needs and providing room to write responses.

The Journey Through Grief is organized around the six needs that all mourners must yield to—indeed embrace—if they are to go on to find continued meaning in life and living. Following a short explanation of each mourning need is a series of brief, spiritual passages that, when read slowly and reflectively, help mourners work through their unique thoughts and feelings.

"The reflections in this book encourage you to think, yes, but to think with your heart and soul," writes Dr. Wolfelt. "They invite you to go to that spiritual place inside you and, transcending our mourning-avoiding society and even your own personal inhibitions about grief, enter deeply into the journey."

Now in softcover, this lovely book is more helpful (and affordable) than ever!

ISBN 978-1-879651-11-1 • 176 pages • softcover • $16.95
(plus additional shipping and handling)

Companion
PRESS

All Dr. Wolfelt's publications can be ordered by mail from:
Companion Press
3735 Broken Bow Road • Fort Collins, CO 80526
(970) 226-6050 • Fax 1-800-922-6051
www.centerforloss.com